GROW YOUR DREAM DENTAL PRACTICE BY DESIGN

10 POWERFUL STRATEGIES TO EXPONENTIALLY GROW YOUR BUSINESS

DR. KINNAR SHAH, BDS.

TRIPLE-CERTIFIED BUSINESS, LEADERSHIP & COMMUNICATIONS COACH

First published in 2020 by Dean Publishing
PO Box 119
Mt. Macedon, Victoria, 3441
Australia
deanpublishing.com

Copyright © Kinnar Shah

All rights reserved. No part of this publication may be reproduced, stored in a retrieval system or transmitted in any way or by any means, electronic, mechanical, photocopying, recording or otherwise, without the prior written permission of the publisher or author.

Cataloguing-in-Publication Data
National Library of Australia
Title: Grow Your Dream Dental Practice By Design
Edition: 2nd edn
ISBN: 978-1-925452-21-1
Category: Business growth/dental industry

The views and opinions expressed in this book are those of the author and do not necessarily reflect the official policy or position of any other agency, publisher, organization, employer or company. Assumptions made in the analysis are not reflective of the position of any entity other than the author(s) — and, these views are always subject to change, revision, and rethinking at any time.

In order to maintain anonymity of certain individuals in some instances names, occupations and places have been changed to protect individuals.
The author, publisher or organizations are not to be held responsible for misuse, reuse, recycled and cited and/or uncited copies of content within this book by others.

GROW YOUR DREAM DENTAL PRACTICE BY DESIGN

10 POWERFUL STRATEGIES TO EXPONENTIALLY GROW YOUR BUSINESS

*To my beautiful wife, Bhavini, who said,
"Your dreams are not for sale."
Thank you for your support and belief in me.*

*To my two children, Mahi and Aveer.
May you both have the courage to live your dreams.*

CONTENTS

Introduction ix

PART 1

The 3 Most Important Skills of a Dentapreneur 1

Business 3

Leadership 9

Communication 41

PART 2

Is Kinnar Crazy? 69

Your Dental Practice Blueprint 77

Four Stages of a Dental Business 85

PART 3

The 10 Best Strategies to Make Your Dental Business Thrive 89

Strategy 1: Marketing 91

Strategy 2: Top Telephone Techniques 117

Strategy 3: Seven-Star Customer Service 125

Strategy 4: Case Conversion 135

Strategy 5: Treatment Coordination… 143

Strategy 6: Follow Up and Follow Through 147

Strategy 7: Referrals and Reviews 155

Strategy 8: Recare 161

Strategy 9: Branding 167

Strategy 10: Your Dental Dashboard 177

Don't Make This The End 181

About Dr Kinnar Shah 189

Acknowledgements 191

End Notes 193

Book References 197

INTRODUCTION

Dear Dentapreneurs,

Deciding to purchase this book may completely alter the way you live and work. Actually, I hope it does. That's why I have written it. To change your business and your life.

Now, that may sound like a massive claim in the first few sentences of this book, but it's not.

Every single strategy, system and idea claimed in this book has been tried-and-tested by hundreds and thousands of dental practitioners; those rebels and misfits that decided to transform the dental industry. I call them Dentapreneurs. They're not your typical dentist. They're not your typical person. They are the new emergence of savvy Dentapreneurs building businesses, brands and empires.

You see, I believe we don't have to do what we've always done. But instead we have to innovate the way things have been done and do them better. That's what evolution is all about, right? Business evolution too.

As you're about to learn, this book is 100% focused on success. YOUR success! On improving your current situation. On giving you more time, more money and more freedom.

My business has been built on these foundations. I do not offer them lightly. They have completely revolutionised my life and the way I think about being a dentist and business owner. I can guarantee if you use these strategies and implement them into your business – you will have a million-dollar *per chair* business. The biggest questions will be, how many chairs do you want?

But these strategies aren't about money, sure they'll make you plenty of money but they'll be more valuable than anything money can buy. Yes, these ideas have successfully generated millions of dollars in revenue for my clients and myself but what they have allowed us to really do is side-step the rat-race and live with choice, by our design, not by default.

You see, dentistry is more than looking in people's mouths all day long. It's more than fixing teeth or giving great smiles. Dentistry is a business based on people, not teeth. It's the people that have teeth. Teeth don't just march into your practice on their own accord. You're in the people business, you're in the business of changing people's lives.

If you think your business is about teeth – you're wrong. A great smile from your client is a by-product of not only what you do, but on how you treat them.

WARNING: The secrets revealed in this book may push you out of your comfort zone. They may require you to think differently, to become a leader and to take control of your business and life. If you don't think you're ready for change, then put down this book now and walk away. This isn't a journey for rigid-thinkers or people stuck in old traditional mindsets. It's designed purely to grow and sustain a thriving business and life.

If you are brave enough to read on, I can guarantee you won't regret reading this book. You will only regret that you didn't read it earlier.

By implementing these strategies, you will do what many dentists don't do – you will build an empire that serves you and your customers. You will work *on* the business more, and *in* the business less. And by doing this, you will be happier, healthier and wealthier. It really is that simple. That's not to say it will be easy. But it won't be hard either.

The 10 strategies in this book are designed to remove any blocks, and erase obstacles that have previously held you back from achieving the next level of success. The roadblocks that have formed and stopped you from having a mind-blowing income, a sustainable business that works when you don't and the exhilarating and exciting life of your dreams.

This system I'm about to share is incredibly powerful. Why?

For 10 major reasons:

1. It works immediately (no set up fees or on-going costs)
2. It doesn't require you to buy anything new (except this book)
3. It's been tried-and-tested (has authentic social proof)
4. It scales (you can grow your business exponentially)
5. It will give you more time
6. It will give you more money
7. It will give you more freedom
8. You'll have less stress and anxiety
9. You'll avoid burnout
10. You will be happier

If you've been struggling to juggle your to-do list and find some time for yourself whilst building your business, I'm here to offer you hope. Real hope. Not false hope.

The American Dental Education Association (ADEA) states that 80% of dental students who graduated in 2016 were at least $100,000 in debt.

In fact, the average debt for dental school students was $261,149.

Now, that's just to be qualified at a dentist. What about starting your own practice?

You've got equipment, rent, insurance, staff and much more on top of that. Not forgetting that along with debt, most new dentists work massively long hours, suffer from high degrees of stress and take very few vacations.

Now, here's the thing. They teach us to become dentists at university. And I'm sure you're pretty damn good at dentistry. But they don't teach you the things you need most. You don't learn anything about running a business, communicating or leadership. Those subjects you usually learn the hard way after university, or like most, you never learn them.

So, this is where this book comes in. This book is jam-packed with all those things you didn't learn but need to learn. This book is not about dentistry. It's about being a Dentapreneur – and I can assure you – those two things are poles apart.

So, if you're ready for a new adventure. If you want to know how I built a successful dental practice by **DESIGN** and not by **DEFAULT**, then keep reading. Things are about to get wild.

Because I'm sure you agree, after all those hours of learning, after all those hours of over-working and living in a pressure-cooker industry – there has to be a better way. And there is. Take the journey with me to find out.

THE #1 COMPLAINT I HEAR FROM DENTISTS

Most dentists I speak with have the same problems. They are overworked, over-stressed, anxious and don't know how to change it.

In fact, many reports back up these legitimate complaints.

In the 2015, a Dentist Health and Wellness Survey from the American Dental Association, showed that 11% of dentists were diagnosed with depression – the rate for the general population that same year was 6.7%.

INTRODUCTION

Also, 6% of dentists were diagnosed with an anxiety disorder, while only 3.1% of the general population were. 4% were identified as suffering from panic attacks, whilst only 2.7% of the general population suffered from panic attacks.

Yes, there is a silent disease running rampant in our dental community. And the only ones who can turn it around is us. Together.

And the effects aren't only mental and emotional. A published 2016 study showed that more than 90%[1] of practicing dentists had back, neck and arm pain. Contorting into unnatural positions for hours on end certainly takes a toll on the human body and brain. I used to have my fair-share of physical pain too.

Now, I could list a myriad of complaints I hear from dentists all over the world. There are many. But my mission is to save you from them. To save you from experiencing the pain – whether it be mental, emotional, physical or financial. I don't want you to live a half-baked existence when you can have it all.

There is a new way.

Burnout in this industry is a very real danger. We must be conscious of the danger that lies within this industry. We must see the danger before it hits. Much like you can see smoke before the fire.

If you're seeing the smoke in your life, if you're already stressed, overworked, experiencing pain physically, mentally or emotionally – then a burning hot fire is on the way.

There's something ready to burn – and I guess that thing is *you*! You will burnout if you continue to do things the 'old way'. You will burnout if you stay as a dentist and don't transition to a Dentapreneur.

Don't be a statistic. Be a leader. Don't allow this industry to lead you – you must lead it!

Now, don't get me wrong, I sympathise. I'm writing this book knowing all too well the issues that occur. How litigation issues are rampant, how

---

1. Al-Mohrej, Omar A et al. "Prevalence of musculoskeletal pain of the neck, upper extremities and lower back among dental practitioners working in Riyadh, Saudi Arabia: a cross-sectional study." BMJ open vol. 6,6 e011100. 20 Jun. 2016, doi:10.1136 /bmjopen-2016-011100

working in confined small spaces all day takes its toll, how being told every day, "I hate seeing you," by well-meaning but anxious clients has its limits. How dealing with missed appointments and panicked people requires a lot more emotional strength than people would know.

Perhaps you're like me, and when you studied at university, you focused on being a great technician, learning your craft and not realising the environment you worked in had other factors than being a good dental technician.

Perhaps you realised that like me, you invested your money in the technical aspect of dentistry and not one cent in learning other skills. Skills and strategies you need the most now but were never taught. You were never taught business skills or correct systems and strategies for increased wellbeing and financial success. It's not your fault! It's how the university system works. They build great dentists but not great business leaders.

So, once I realised that I lacked the skills I needed most. I became hellbent on getting them. Obsessed. I consumed more books, courses and leaderships programs in a few years that most people do their entire life. I became absorbed in education. Personal and business education. The education I needed to become successful. It transformed everything, including me.

And this education is what you will find in every page of this book. The education I was given that turned me from a dental employee to a dental owner, to a Dentapreneur. I want you to have the same joy and success that I have found.

So, what is this system that sounds too good to be true?

I am going to outline **10 proven strategies** for you to implement into your business. Strategies designed to change the direction of your business. Strategies all about how you can design your destiny and be the captain of your own ship.

But before I deliver these 10 strategies, it's important to add this: if you love being a dentist and have no ambition in growing an empire, don't despair. Although this book focuses on growing dental practices, it also adds the elements of customer service, leadership, communication, selling, landing new clients and handling common dental problems. In short, even if you don't want to grow an empire, just by learning these strategies you will become a better dentist, a happier dentist and one that can see the smoke before the fire. There's really nothing to lose and everything to gain.

CHOICE IS THE ULTIMATE FREEDOM

Let me ask you this: Do you want to holiday in the Caribbean or in Europe?

Do you want to send your kids to a private school or a public school? Do you want to take a day off when you want or only on a public holiday? Do you want to spend the weekends not thinking about work and enjoying your time off?

The answers really don't matter.

It doesn't matter if you want to holiday in the Caribbean or Europe. It doesn't matter if your kids go to a public school or a private school. What matters the most is that YOU HAVE THE CHOICE.

Choice is freedom. Choice allows *you* to decide. To craft your life rather than let life push you around. You get to decide what you want to do.

I have seen way too many dentists being pushed around by the demands of their business, the demands of customers, the demands of their staff. And it's not supposed to be like that.

You see, we are all given the power of choice but sometimes we don't exercise our own rights to it.

I want you to imagine two dentists. They both have the same education and the same opportunities. They have the same motivation and the same focus. One is building a thriving business, whereas the other is still paying off debt. One is happy, one is stressed.

What's the difference between them?

Though they both have the same amount of focus and the same amount of time. The difference is one dentist knows where to apply his/her focus and the other doesn't. One focused their time and their team's time on *working* strategies and systems. The other one tried to work on any and all strategies.

The successful one didn't try to focus his attention on everything, he couldn't. He only focused on tried-and-tested, *working* strategies.

You see, you can't afford to focus on the wrong things. The statistics are damn ugly.

Most businesses in Australia fail to thrive. Professor Colin McLeod – Program Director, Master of Entrepreneurship in the Faculty of Business and Economics at University of Melbourne reports that 97% of startup businesses "will either exit or fail to grow".

And of that, 60% of small businesses stop operation within the first three years of their startup journey.[2]

But the real interesting thing isn't the amount that fail. The most important thing to know is WHY they fail. How can so many people fail at business? And the answer makes sense.

The Australian Centre for Business Growth investigated why businesses were failing at such rapid rates. Their new research identifies the reasons Australian small and medium-sized businesses are failing.[3]

The data was collected from CEOs who had been part of a company failure or whose small or medium companies had failed. And what they found were the top reasons they failed.

---

2. Australian Bureau of Statistics: www.abs.gov.au
3. 2018, New study reveals why Australian SMEs fail, Australian Centre for Business Growth, University of South Australia Business School, 20 November 2018, www.unisa.edu.au/Media-Centre/Releases/2018/new-study-reveals-why-australian-smes-fail

TOP REASONS FOR SMALL TO MEDIUM BUSINESS FAILURE

25% – Insufficient leadership and management and planning and execution.

17% – Inadequate market research, marketing, sales

14% – Poor financial management

13% – Underestimating the impact of externalities

11% – Poor governance structures re: partners, family

7% – Product or service problems

6% – Poor management of people

4% – Inexperienced CEO

3% – Wrong strategy or poor implementation

TOTAL = 100%

Source: Data collected by the Australian Centre for Business Growth at the University of South Australia's Business School (2014 – 2018). Used with permission.

So, I'm going to repeat myself again. You don't fail at being a good dentist. If your business isn't successful it *isn't* due to your technical skill. It's due to the lack of business skill and customer skill.

And that's what you're going to be given right now. I am going to condense my hard-earned knowledge and deliver it to you in under 300 pages. If I do my job right, you will begin to implement things immediately.

YOU WILL DO WHAT OTHER BUSINESSES FAIL TO DO!

We will focus ONLY on what works. You will focus on what you NEED to focus on to be successful.

Australia has around 2.1 million small businesses, which accounts for about 97% of all businesses registrations nationally. A new small business is created every 100 seconds.[4]

---

4. Stache Magazine, Oct 15 2019, 'How Many Small Business Fail in Australia'. Small Business Magazine, https://stachemagazine.com/how-many-small-business-fail-in-australia

Yet, most fail because they don't have the RIGHT information about what it takes to be successful.

This book isn't for carpenters or real-estate agents or other career paths that take up on job market. This is for you, my fellow comrades in dentistry. We are a unique bunch. We understand the problems and pitfalls of our industry. I have been in the trenches too, and I can tell you the way out. I know dentists. I talk with them every single day. I run workshops only for dentists.

This is why I am calling for us to get savvy, get smarter than our fancy degree. It's time for us to get business smart, people smart and go out there and disrupt the industry in a positive way. Dental disruptors unite! And the reason I'm saying this is because there's plenty of room for a positive disruption.

The BOQ Specialist Dental Practice Research Report 2016/17[5] found that while three in four dentists want to improve their practice and profitability, only 33% have the ability to properly assess their performance results and know the areas for improvement.

As I said, it's what we focus on that matters.

The report included one-on-one interviews with dentists of mid-sized practices. These businesses turned over between $1.5m and $3.5m. Yet, here's the kicker: 77% of the dentists surveyed agreed that their practices were not operating at peak efficiency and only 41% of them had a plan to address this.

In other words, nearly half didn't want to even look at why their business wasn't running at its peak. They are quite content to sit back and let the business turn over its usual amount without looking closer. How long do you think that will last?

68% of the dentists admitted they didn't have a plan for the future of their business.

---

5. BOQ Specialist, Dental Practice Research Report 2016/17, www.boqspecialist.com.au/expertise/dental-research-report

So, in this uncertain business climate and with an unprecedented number of new dentists emerging from uni every day. What will happen to these businesses?

Though they may be enjoying their turnover, without a plan and without a need to look at their business productivity and efficiency – many will decline. You can't stay complacent and expect excellence.

But for those who don't put their head in the sand, for those willing to do what others fail to do; for those leaders, the world and all its riches are yours.

The fascinating thing about this survey is that it revealed a dentist's strengths and weaknesses. It said dentists are "highly intelligent, highly educated and self-motivated individuals". It revealed that dentists have strong values in relation to patient care, and these values extend beyond making money. I agree.

Yet, the study also reported many dentists feel burdened by the toughening economic conditions and worry about patient growth and the threat posed by corporatisation and health-fund preferred provider arrangements.

Most failed to plan or even look at what makes their business successful or not.

It's NOT your lack of motivation, or lack of education. It's about what I call the **Dental Blueprint of Success**. You need this blueprint, much like you need a roadmap when driving into new unchartered territory.

I'd like for you to consider this your **Dental Blueprint of Success**. Your roadmap to plan and build a business beyond the 'norm'. Be outrageously abnormal and do what the other dentists fail to do, and you'll never fail.

Watch your *thoughts*,
they become words.

Watch your *words*,
they become actions.

Watch your *actions*,
they become habits.

Watch your *habits*,
they become your character.

Watch your *character*,
it becomes your
DESTINY.

PART 1

THE 3 MOST IMPORTANT SKILLS OF A DENTAPRENEUR

Before we go head-first into The Dental Blueprint of Success, there are some very important areas we must address first. Because like anything in life, you can have the roadmap to success but you also have to take a good look at yourself. You may have the map that leads you to gold but if you don't know what gold looks like or you don't have the skill to recognise it, you'll walk straight past it.

From my experience, most dentists put the cart before the horse. They build a business before they build themselves. Many, in fact, never look within for ways to improve. But I'm going to tell you honestly, the good ones, the great ones... they ALL do this. And they never stop growing and developing as leaders and people.

These are the 3 most important skills you will need if you want to experience exponential business growth. Do not try to skip these, because at some stage along your journey, they'll save your ass. You cannot become great without them. Period.

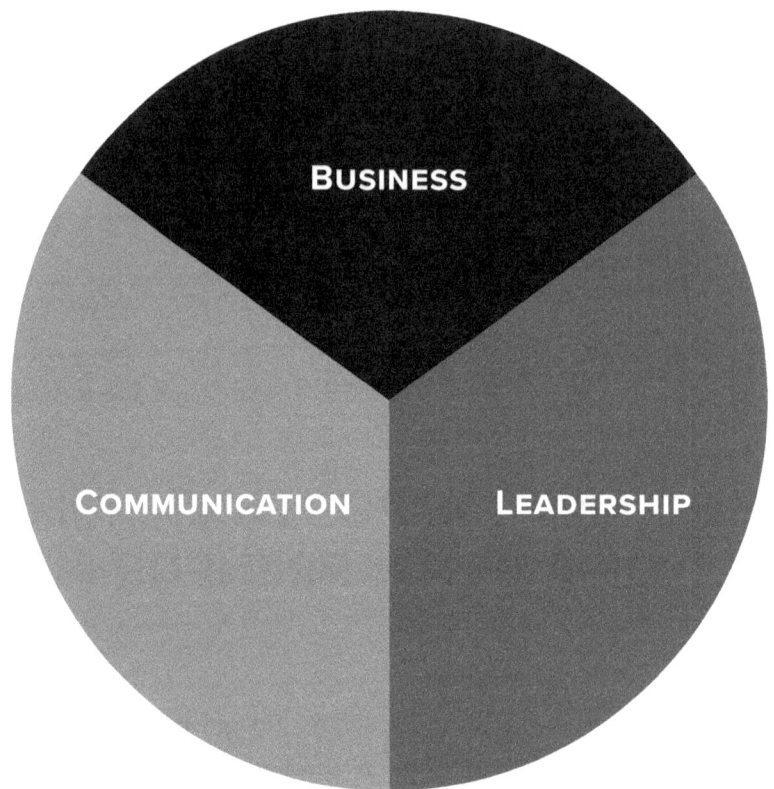

To be the best you can be you will need knowledge in these three areas:

BUSINESS, LEADERSHIP and COMMUNICATION.

BUSINESS

When it comes to running and building a business, knowledge is power. Or more to the point, the *right* knowledge is power.

Scientists have worked out exactly how much data is sent to a typical person's brain every day. The study conducted by researchers at the University of California in San Diego, suggests that people are flooded with the equivalent amount of 34 Gb (gigabytes) of information.[6] To put this in perspective, this daily amount is enough to overload a laptop within a week.

Every day people receive over 105,000 words into their brain.

So, with all this overload of information, what to focus on becomes essential. (I dive into this deeply in the following chapters).

✘ If you focus on the wrong strategies for your dental practice, it won't last.

✓ If you focus on the right things, it will grow.

I have done the work for you. I am giving you the essential information you need to focus on in order to build your dental practice. I promise

---

6. Bohn, Roger & Short, James. (2012). Measuring Consumer Information. *International Journal of Communication*. 6. 980-1000.

you. It's that simple.

With the continual overload of social media, blogs, articles, news feeds, newspapers, magazines, books and conversation, it's important that we manage the knowledge we receive. That we intentionally manage what we focus on and learn from, and what we don't.

Three key reasons why actively managing knowledge is important to a company's success are:
1. It helps us make the right decisions on what we focus on and what we don't
2. It helps build your business efficiently
3. It stimulates continual growth and innovation

Business knowledge is essential to growing your dental business. You simply cannot put your head in the sand and expect results. It doesn't work that way. But it doesn't mean you need to know absolutely everything there is to know about building a business, that is a lifelong journey and changes over time and seasons. But you do need to know certain things, or have staff that know certain things.

You will need to know how to manage your finances, how to build a team, how to communicate effectively and how to be a leader.

This book will teach you about business in a way that is *relevant* to you and your dental practice.

You will learn:
- The Four Stages a dental practice goes through and how to identify them
- The 10 Strategies designed to gain 80% of your results
- The 3 essential skills of a Dentapreneur
- How to build a million-dollar per chair business
- How to market your business easily

And most importantly you will also notice what I won't be teaching you. I will not be focusing on other types of practices – this is specifically for dentists. I won't be focusing on stocks and shares and budgets. I won't be telling you when to buy your dental practice and in which suburb.

The reason is, this book is intentionally designed to manage your knowledge, to give you the strategies that have been specifically hand-picked by someone who has been there and done that. The knowledge that has been crystallised and distilled to give you the most effective and immediate RESULTS!

You see, results speak more than anything in business. You get results and everyone wants to know how you did it. You get results and your business booms. You get results and you feel proud of what you have achieved.

True business knowledge isn't just about gathering information. True business knowledge is a proven system of knowledge designed to get RESULTS.

GET YOUR HANDS DIRTY

When it comes to business knowledge you must get involved. Your accountant or financial planner is NOT your CFO. They are paid to give you financial literacy. Unfortunately, most business owners don't understand this until it's too late and are often left wondering why they didn't become financially literate.

If you go into business for yourself, you are responsible for your business. If you don't know something (which of course you can't know everything) – then of course, you need to hire experts too. But hiring experts does not mean you hand responsibility to them. It's always your responsibility.

Richard Branson said he had four tips to growing a successful business on his Virgin website recently.[7] "It is no easy task but with the right

---

7. 2015, Interview by Natalie Clarkson, *Richard Branson: My four tips for growing a business*, 3 June 2015, Virgin.com, www.virgin.com/entrepreneur/richard-branson-my-four-tips-growing-business

support and a smart approach, the dream of scaling up your venture from start-up to successful business is in reach."

These are his tips.

Have a Long-term Plan, Goals, Roadmap
"Setting some milestones for you and your team to work towards will keep you motivated and driven […] There will be obstacles to growth you cannot foresee but having a roadmap in place from the get-go will help build structure and focus to decision-making."

Stick to Your Principles
He encourages business owners to look closely at their business values and principles early on. These values and principles can then be converted into tangible activities and meaning your customers can interact with.

Get a Great Team
Invest in your people and let them do their job. He said, "There is little point recruiting great people if you don't then give them the autonomy to take their role and run with it." He says recruiting the right people has freed him up. "Over my 40 years in business I have assembled a fantastic team to run the Virgin Group's day-to-day activities and this has freed me up to spend 80 per cent of my time working with Virgin Unite – the not-for-profit arm of the Virgin Group."

Get Great Support
Get support, mentors, good advice. He said, "I myself benefited hugely from the words of Sir Freddie Laker when starting Virgin Atlantic. He told me I could never compete with the big advertising budgets of the large airlines and would have to get out there and use myself to promote Virgin Atlantic."

Most dentist's brains are filled with teeth. Okay, not literally, that would be bizarre. But we think about teeth and how to be the best

PART 1: BUSINESS

dentist. We go to courses to learn about the latest equipment and the latest techniques and technology. But we need to change our brains.

Unless you make a change in you. A change in your choices. A change in your cranium. You won't obtain a change in your circumstances.

I encourage people to upgrade their brain. Many are the first to upgrade their phone or update their car…but how many are committed to upgrading their mental and emotional skills?

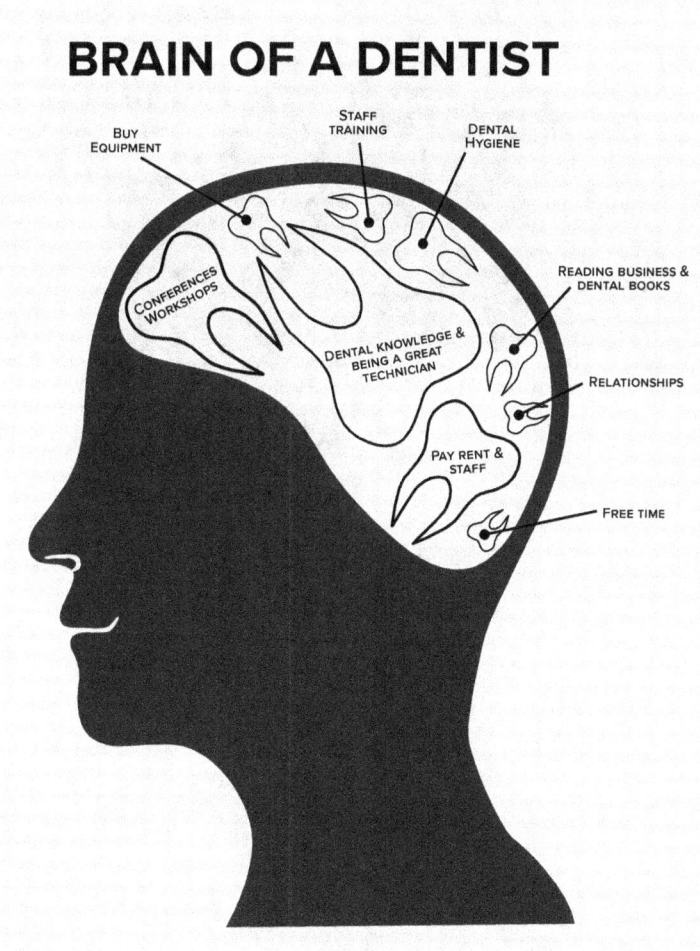

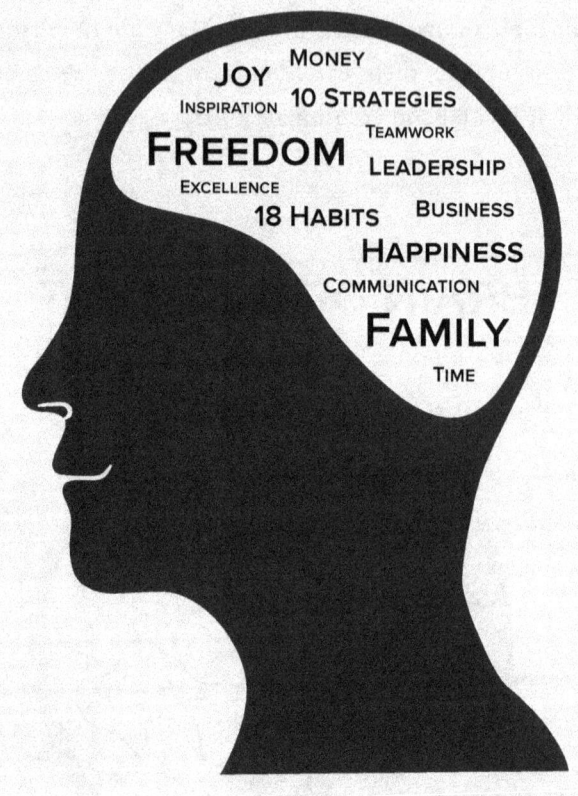

LEADERSHIP

"If your actions inspire others to dream more, learn more, do more and become more, you are a leader."
John Quincy Adams

Most dentists think of themselves as a dentist. Don't. Dentistry is a skill that you have. Much like you have other skills, maybe you're a great golfer or exceptionally good at crosswords. Being a dentist is a profession, you may even retire from doing it one day. But being a leader is for life.

Focusing on leadership will make you a better dentist. But focusing only on dentistry will not make you a leader.

Leaders are not born, they're made. No one is born leading. In fact, the closest percentage research teams have come up with is that at least 70% of leadership is a learned skill. Whether this percentage can truly be known is yet to be seen.

The reason why leaders are made, not born is because people can become leaders through the process of teaching, learning, experience and observation. Leadership is a set of skills that can be learned through training, practice and experience over time. Leadership skills develop all through life. Great leaders are the ones that actively seek out to hone and craft these skills.

A study conducted by the University of Illinois found that leadership can be learned in as little as 15 weeks.[8] The researchers compared the process of becoming a leader to that of a three-legged stool, saying the three legs of "being ready, willing and able," must happen first.

First, students would need to be *ready* to learn. Then, they must have the *willingness* to learn. Finally, they become *able* when they have both the skills and motivation to lead.

One of the authors of the study, David Rosch defines leadership like this:

> *"Leadership is an individual influencing a group of people toward a common goal. So how do you influence people? You can lead through your interactions, your relationships, your communication, the way you express thanks, your ethics."*

So, leadership is a broad set of skills that enables you to inspire, influence and impact.

And in order to achieve this I believe we need to obtain good habits. Make leadership a habit. If you look at all the great leaders of the world, they all had habits they did every day that shaped them.

> *"Wouldn't it be great to be gifted? In fact, ... It turns out that choices lead to habits. Habits become talents. Talents are labelled gifts. You're not born this way, you get this way."*
> **Seth Godin**

---

8. Journal of Leadership Education, *Developmental Readiness for Leadership: The Differential Effects of Leadership Courses on Creating "Ready, Willing, and Able" Leader*, https://aces.illinois.edu

HABITS CAN MAKE OR BREAK YOU

Did you know that around 40% of everything you do on a daily basis is *habitual*?

This means that nearly half of our day and our lives are entirely on autopilot! Now, if you have good habits, then you're on the path to success. But if you have habits that don't support your success, then the news isn't so good.

Evaluate your habits. Are they supporting you toward your dreams or are they taking you away from them?

Here's something important you must know about habits:

Unless you consciously use your will power to create something new, your present habits are creating your future life for you.

By default, your brain will go for the path of least resistance. It will play the old habits you have unless you deliberately create new ones.

Habits come in many forms. For example, there are:

- **Action habits** – when we sleep and wake, when we shower, what, when and how we eat and drink, how we spend our time, when and how we exercise (or don't).
- **Mental habits** – such as how we think about ourselves, how we talk about ourselves inside, what we believe and create stories about. How we perceive others or how we view certain situations. What we tend to focus on or not.
- **Feeling habits** – We also have habitual patterns of feeling, or things that habitually triggers feelings for us.

Habits actually help form structure to our lives. And if you choose habits that serve you and are aligned with your future vision – life can get very good. Choose poor habits and there will be consequences to those choices.

Bestselling author and entrepreneur Brendan Burchard studied high performance habits, these studies led him to interview, research and coach, some of the world's most successful people from CEOs to athletes and entertainers, to even 1.6 million students from 195 countries.

He has shown that by using the right habits, anyone can get phenomenal results and become a high achiever in any industry. That includes dentistry!

High performance is not achieved by a particular type of person, but by specific habits and rituals.

> *"Study high performers and you will see that they have systems built into their days that drive their success."*
> ***Brendan Burchard***
> ***High Performance Habits***

And it's true, habits create rituals and routines and these create discipline and character. As Bruce Lee said, "I fear not the man who has practiced 10,000 kicks, but I do fear the man who has practiced one kick 10,000 times."

This is what the right habits do. Habits that are honed give a human, superhuman powers. They focus energy in a powerful and deliberate way.

I consider there are 18 essential habits to being a great leader.

THE 18 ESSENTIAL HABITS TO BECOMING A GREAT LEADER

1. Habit of Self-Knowledge

> *"Knowing yourself is the beginning of all wisdom."*
> *Aristotle*

Self-knowledge is more critical than ever. It's important to slow down, breathe and reflect, rather than get swept up in the rat race of life.

Self-awareness and self-knowledge increases as speed decreases. Know and respect your own strengths, limitations and values. Learn to assess yourself and gain insight. Things like personal development courses, retreats and the Gallup StrengthsFinder[9] are very helpful.

The more you "know thyself" the better leader you become.

2. Habit of Transparency

> *"Keep your mind open to change all the time. Welcome it. Court it. It is only by examining and re-examining your opinions and ideas that you can progress."*
> *Dale Carnegie*

Be open and transparent, show and share your vulnerabilities and failures. Embrace your life lessons. Authentic leaders have the strength to admit when they've made a mistake and take they take steps to solve it. Make honesty and trust the standard for your organisation. It all starts with you. Transparency is the new black, it's important to remain a congruent open-minded leader.

3. Habit of Shepherding

> *"Get obsessed with something that can provide value to others, that can lift and inspire others towards their own greatness."*
> *Kinnar Shah*

---

9. www.gallup.com/press/176429/strengthsfinder.aspx

It's not all about you! Ask yourself this – is your workplace too dependent on you? Do you receive criticism as regularly as you offer it to others?

A great leader is a team player. They hire the right people, put them in the right roles and give them resources they need, and then they get out of their way. Great leaders make everyone around them better. A great leader says "we" not "me". Every business is a reflection of its leader.

Great leaders influence with positive and inspirational energy, not domination and control. A great leader shepherds others from trouble and guides them to solutions.

4. Habit of Character-Building

> *"It's the repetition of affirmations that leads to belief.*
> *And once that belief becomes a deep conviction,*
> *things begin to happen."*
> *Muhammad Ali*

Who are you when no one is looking?

The best leaders are the ones that build character before building their ego. It's often in those little moments that no one else sees that determine one's character. True leaders always get tested at some point and it's in these moments that the opportunity to form your character lies. Those times when you need to make the right decision versus the popular decision, or pick up the slack after hours or do the not so glamourous work behind the scenes. A true leader doesn't shy away from character building moments but uses them to find new resources within.

5. Habit of Attention

> *"The leader is the person who brings a*
> *little magic to the moment."*
> *Denise Morrison*
> *President & CEO, Campbell Soup*

Mindfulness is about "being mindful", about having greater awareness of the present moment. Mindfulness is the art of experiencing the present moment for what it is. It's about not being reactive but experiencing life. Small moments are big opportunities – things like listening, paying attention to your practice, observing and being in the moment, not the past or future. Placing your attention on the present moment and doing what is needed in the moment brings a sprinkling of magic to that moment.

6. Habit of Igniting Your Calling

> *"Everybody has a calling. And your real job in life is to figure out as soon as possible what that is, who you were meant to be, and to begin to honour that in the best way possible for yourself."*
> ***Oprah Winfrey***

What is your purpose? What are you supposed to do?

Everybody has a purpose. Everybody has a calling. The wisdom is to discover and connect with it so it can lead you. Some people get muddled and erroneously wrap their entire identity around their occupation believing that is who they are, but it's not, it's only what they do for a living. Who you are and what you do sit together in harmony to give you the ultimate avenue to express your passion. Congruent alignment between who we are and what we do helps us serve, express and fulfil our deepest passion. Find it and use it with vigour.

My calling is to influence the influencers. I sense that I'm called to gather, connect, equip and inspire leaders who are making a difference in the world. To ignite passion and energy in others.

7. Habit of Ambition

Ambition is a driving force in many people's lives. Leaders tend to be very ambitious. They set goals, they strive for results, they aim to grow and deliver. However, there is healthy ambition and selfish ambition.

Healthy ambition is about growing and reaching new heights and taking everyone with you for the ride.

Selfish ambition blinds people and can result in people being used for personal gain or success. Selfish leadership is a short road, usually there are broken promises everywhere because people were useful; until they weren't.

Great leadership isn't getting work done through people, it's growing people through work.

8. Habit of Curiosity

> *"The important thing is to not stop questioning. Curiosity has its own reason for existing."*
> **Albert Einstein**

As children, we're naturally curious – it's how we grow and learn. Yet have you noticed that as we grow older, our sense of wonder starts to dwindle? Regaining our sense of curiosity is important to our success. Curious people are always seeking new ideas, new knowledge, new ways of doing things.

Curious people are always engaging in new conversations and stay open-minded to possibilities. They seek new opportunities and explore new horizons. As Einstein said, "I have no special gift. I am only passionately curious," and "never lose a holy curiosity".

9. Habit of Passionate Purpose

> *"One of the huge mistakes people make is that they try to force an interest on themselves. You don't choose your passions; your passions choose you."*
> **Jeff Bezos**
> **Founder & CEO, Amazon**

Passionate purpose is a dynamic force within you. It's what keeps you going when everything else is against you. Passionate purpose is an internal driving force that helps you stand back up and try all over again despite oncoming obstacles. Passion is a flame that once lit can remain burning bright when the shadows are dark and gloomy.

Without passionate purpose, you are simply doing a job. With passionate purpose, you are changing lives and adding value to people.

Purposeful passion will get you out of bed even on the days you don't feel like it. It will push you beyond your comfort zone and beg you to expand your horizons and look for new possibilities to become a leader and a changemaker. Passionate purpose is not just a feeling, it's the fuel that drives your doingness and stretches you to be more, give more, add more — become more! It's like explosive dynamite once it's set alight within you.

10. Habit of Creativity

"Innovation distinguishes between a leader and a follower."
Steve Jobs
Apple co-founder

It's important to stay current and creative. Good leaders make this a habit. And the key to innovation is to be intentional about it.

I soon realised that being intentional requires:

1. **Courage:** to leap into unchartered terrain and take risks.
2. **Disappointment:** a willingness to have one or several disappointments.
3. **Determination:** the ability to push through the painful moments and quitting stages.
4. **Inspiration:** allowing room for sparking inspiring new thoughts and ideas that also ignite innovation and collaboration.

These 4 elements: Courage, Disappointment, Determination and Inspiration will ignite innovation and keep it ignited if you're intentional about building this habit.

11. Habit of Vision

"Although my circumstance was homeless, my vision wasn't!"
Eric Thomas

Many great visionaries have something major in common — they set their gaze far into the future and inspire others to see the same hope, the same dream, the same opportunities and common goal. This depth of spirit allows us to be hopeful instead of hopeless, powerful instead of powerless, driven to achieve instead of driven into despair. Inspiring a great vision gives daily work and daily challenges meaning and purpose.

Being a visionary leader is one of today's most necessary requirements. Being able to captivate, cast and communicate a great vision busts old archaic behaviours and allows for new and exciting possibilities and opportunities. Recognising this deeper part of the human spirit can leaders soar to new heights and spark entire movements. Think of Martin Luther King Jnr, Gandhi and Nelson Mandela's great vision.

Once you discover your own unique vision, you can develop and learn how to communicate it regularly and clearly so that others will also be moved to head in the same incredible direction.

Bestselling author and visionary Simon Sinek tweeted this:

> *"If you hire people just because they can do a job, they'll work for your money. But if you hire people who believe what you believe, they'll work for you with blood and sweat and tears."*

People want to be part of an adventure, we all desire to make a mark, and we long to be part of something significant that stretches and astonishes us. Inspiring leaders create a vision, a mission and a cause way bigger than themselves so that others can own, follow, be inspired by, and be a part of it too.

12. HABIT OF COURAGE

> *"Whatever you can do or dream you can, begin it;*
> *Boldness has genius, power, and magic in it."*
> **Johann Wolfgang von Goethe**

It's important to stay courageous amongst the storms, to be bold in taking calculated risks. Being bold is the ability to do something that frightens you.

Being bold is not the absence of fear but rather the willingness to face the dark storms and overcome them.

Starting my own venture was quite the gamble. Having just left an organisation in its prime, I was a commodity. But if I launched my own endeavour and it flopped, I might not recover. This could ruin me I thought. I'm a big believer in taking risks, but I must admit, it was difficult to take my own medicine with so much on the line. It wasn't swimming with Great White sharks, but it did require embracing the unknown. And no one likes to do that. Anxiety swirled. Prayers rolled.

Time ticked. Everyday bravery wavered. Boldness can be the medicine we need when fear makes us feel sick.

It's been said that you find the magic outside of your comfort zone, and I believe this is true. But to do this, we need to muster courage, even if we have to discover it from unknown places. After all that's what courage is all about, drawing up inner resources in order to face something or do something we're not convinced we can quite yet do. Courage is the antidote to fear.

> *"Do not follow where the path may lead. Go instead*
> *where there is no path and leave a trail."*
> *Ralph Waldo Emerson*

13. Habit of High Standards

> *"Excellence is never an accident. It is always the result of high intention, sincere effort, and intelligent execution; it represents the wise choice of many alternatives – choice, not chance, determines your destiny."*
> ***Aristotle***

When I get hired as a consultant or a coach to evaluate and bring the best out in someone or in their business, I feel they often expect me to act like a business school professor. They wait to hear my feedback and expect a detailed explanation of how they should restructure their entire business and lives. My biggest advice consists of only 3 words – STOP BEING AVERAGE.

Set standards that scare you. If you're going to sweep the floor– sweep as if Michelangelo painted it.

Developing high standards often requires you to set a standard that even worries you, it can induce a feeling that flows between thrilling and slightly scary. Some people think setting high standards means being as good as the next guy. But being the best and pursuing excellence isn't about being big or having the largest budget or costly expense accounts. High standards are ultimately about effort. Often your comfort zone is your danger zone.

High standards help a leader and an organisation move from average to exceptional, from good to great. What are the standards you can turn into benchmarks? How can you begin pointing to the farthest and biggest goals and then motivate you and your team to get there? These are the practices that will make your organisation unique and force your average competitors to begin mimicking you rather than the other way around.

High standards in business can be boiled down to four things:

1. **Be Efficient:** Do work well and within the right timeframes
2. **Be Effective:** Use systems that streamline processes
3. **Be Excellent:** Set a code of excellence across all areas
4. **Be Congenial:** Be a pleasure to work with.

14. HABIT OF NEVER GIVING UP

> *"It's not that I'm so smart, it's just that I stay with problems longer."*
> **Albert Einstein**

A great business and becoming a great leader is a product of perseverance. It's about putting practises in place and riding the highs and lows that accompany all businesses at some stage.

Quite often the success goes to the one that continues on despite obstacles, the one that looks for solutions and ways forward when blockages appear.

If it wasn't for this habit, many of our most incredible inventions would never have seen the light of day. Cultivating the habit of not giving up isn't easy if you've been used to giving up the first moment things get a little tough, but if you stay with it and find new ways to sit in the discomfort, things always change.

Thomas A. Edison has been described as America's greatest inventor, in fact not only did he invent the electric power system and bring electricity into our homes but he also created the motion picture industry, the recording industry, the X-ray machine, and even the tattoo pen. When trying to master the invention of the light bulb Edison allegedly said, "I have not failed 1,000 times. I have successfully discovered 1,000 ways to NOT make a light bulb." That's the best attitude!

According to the Edison Innovation Foundation (thomasedison.org), he built this attitude on four simple principles taught to him by his beloved mother.

These are:
1. Never get discouraged if you fail. Learn from it. Keep trying.
2. Learn with both your head and hands.
3. Not everything of value in life comes from books – experience the world.
4. Never stop learning. Read the entire panorama of literature.[10]

These four attitudes can carry you very very far.

15. Habit of Finishing

"You can't build a reputation on what you're going to do."
Henry Ford

Some people conveniently slip into the middle of the pack, they work just hard enough to keep their jobs and fly under the radar. But if you want to become a great leader, you must decide to do the things most people don't do. Finishing jobs to completion is one of these things. And, let's be honest, it's becoming a rare thing to find these days. How many people do you know who allow themselves to be constantly distracted? How many people do you know who never finish what they start? I bet it's a lot. Don't be like them.

When you're tempted to slack off or slow down, outwork everyone else. When you're being seduced into complacency, take stock of yourself and decide you won't allow complacency to live inside of you. Strong leaders accomplish things, they see things through to the end without bailing out when the going gets tough. They get things done. Period.

Develop the habit of finishing, of being there right to the end. Execute! Slay the painful procrastinating voice that lives inside of you. Don't listen to its petty whines and promises — it's trying to lure you into stopping your mission, into the 'safe, soft place' of complacency. Don't fall for this temptation. Exceute every time. Not once but always.

---

10. www.edisonmuckers.org/thomas-edisons-philosophy

Finish what you start and make this the bedrock of your leadership. Finishing never fails!

16. Habit of Appreciating Others

> *"The strength of the team is each individual member.*
> *The strength of each member is the team."*
> ***Phil Jackson***

Google has mastered a principle that the rest of us would do well to learn: when you prioritise your team, your team will prioritise you. How well do you treat your people? Do you honour them, appreciate them, find ways to make their lives better? Or do you only care about what they can do for you — to make you money or increase efficiency or perform a function? If you objectify others, they will reciprocate the same way.

How do you describe your team members? Money makers? Numbers on a spreadsheet/payroll? A good analogy for your team might be *family*.

Cultivate a culture that motivates and values people. All leaders can find ways to love and appreciate their people and help their people build relationships with each other. Do this and you won't just build a better work family; you'll open the door to greater success.

One great question I have heard in leadership conferences is to ask – *What's it like to be on the other side of me?*

This is a superb question to ask yourself and reflect on. The insight you gain from asking yourself this question is priceless.

After all, leadership is not the position you hold, it's really the inspiration you spread and the influence you have. Decide to be the leader you always dreamed of being. Be that mentor for others and they will appreciate you beyond the norm. Why? Because true leadership is about doing things beyond the norm, caring for others beyond their mere job description. It's a daily choice and behaviour to be an empowering influence.

17. Habit of Partnerships

"Alone we can do so little; together we can do so much."
Helen Keller

Partnerships, collaborations, joint ventures are all powerful relationships to include in your circle of business life. Some of the most innovative and exciting products or services only exist because many minds went to work on a vision together.

The famous saying, 'no man is an island' has a lot of truth to it. Given the fact, we don't even enter the world by ourselves should be enough for people to register that humans naturally bond and collaborate in order to further humanity. In business, having a mindset that is open to partnerships and collaboration is a healthy one. Many new businesses need to partner before they can power on and make significant progress.

Truth is, if you could get there on your own, you would already be there, right?

Now, I'm not saying to go out and partner with just anyone, that would be irresponsible and possibly dangerous to your business. But be open to authentic and mutually beneficial partnerships that progress both sides. Win-win scenarios.

Think about the most revolutionary items you interact with every day of your life.

Your car? A television set? A laptop? A smartphone? Think about common cooking utensils or even this book. Most inventions or innovations are created via partnerships in some way. Even you! You're the product of a partnership.

When you value others and want to create win-win partnerships with people, you create a bigger circle of influence, and part of your responsibility is to share that bigger circle and its benefits with others.

True collaboration involves giving as much as getting. Here's a thought: even Microsoft and Apple collaborated.

18. Habit of Small Shifts

"Success is a few simple disciplines, practiced every day; while failure is simply a few errors in judgment, repeated every day."
Jim Rohn

Tony Robbins' golf coach is a man called Tim Hurja. Tim Hurja introduced Tony Robbins to the concept of the 2-Millimetre Shift. He said, "In golf your clubface must be square to the path you're swinging on to hit the ball straight, it's less than a 2-millimetre shift that makes all the difference." He said, "a two-millimetre shift may not seem like much, but as you carry that small shift out further and further it has a dramatic impact on your outcome."[11]

If you think about it, a two-millimetre inaccuracy ends up as metres and metres off the target in the long run. Or vice versa, small pivots in the right direction, end up very close to your target in the long run. Small shifts make big differences.

I have experienced much success in my career but for a while there I stopped prioritising time for the activities I enjoyed because everything was "urgent". As a result, I forfeited exercise, I ate poorly and suffered from lack of sleep. Stopping to slow down allowed me to get my smile back.

Some people like to wear a badge of "busyness". They like to the busy entrepreneur that is overworked and overwhelmed. It can portray an image of "success". It comes with a silent mantra that says, "I'm really busy." What if the mantra was "I'm resting and reflecting"? Our mantra is usually "I'm really busy." What if our mantra was *"I'm rested and rejuvenated"*?

Taking time off seems like falling behind, or losing the edge of your game. Even peers within your organisation might think you're lazy or just looking for an excuse to take more time away. When you feel caught on

---

11. Bill Carmody, Published online August 22, 2016, www.billcarmody.com/tony-robbins-explains-2-millimeter-shift-can-make-break-business

the treadmill of running fast and long distances to "get ahead" — you're going to burnout. If you're not willing to stop, rest and reflect, you will crash and burn. You must pivot in a healthier direction and make small shifts in a direction that allows you to go the distance without burning out. Small shifts make big differences.

For businesses, even small margins can create great profit.

For all of us, time is our greatest asset. We can't create more of it. We have to make sure we are using it wisely, and small shifts allows us to leverage time effectively

All leaders need to know time management and how to build and look for shifts in both their personal and professional lives.

3 LEADERSHIP HABITS YOU CAN BEGIN TO USE IMMEDIATELY

These 18 habits are, in fact, the basis of my two-day workshop. We go into great detail and form strategies for implementing leadership into our lives. As the 18 Habits are really a book in themselves, I will discuss three in greater detail to give you something immediate to implement. As I said at the beginning, this is a book of action, not just reading.

The top three traits of leadership we will delve into are humbleness, hunger and hustle. These were first introduced to me through a great book called *H3 Leadership: Be Humble. Stay Hungry. Always Hustle* by Brad Lomenick. I loved them so much that I began to implement them in my life and they became a part of me too.

Now I tell people that there are many powerful habits to cultivate but if you're not ready to commit to a series of excellent habits yet, then just begin with these three and life will explode with new opportunities anyway. In summary: leaders need to stay humble, have the deep drive of hunger and the ability to hustle.

Here's my personal take on these three habits.

1. H – Humbleness

Many leaders are mission-minded. They focus on goals, tasks and achievement and that's how they've ended up with influence. Many leaders are mission-minded. They focus on goals, tasks and achievement and that's how they become known for their focus and influence.

Some leaders, however, become so narrowly focused on their goals that they overlook people and purpose. Some become too inflated with ambition that they step on others in order to progress.

To curb an over-inflated mission-minded tendency requires a good dose of humbleness. Without a firm foundation of humbleness; power and influence can leak into unethical behaviours or abusing a position of power.

Humble leaders are leaders that give credit to others and thinks beyond their position of power. They are willing to take feedback and learn from mistakes. They keep their hearts humble and thankful.

Some people think that leadership entails someone on an ego-trip wanting to control others, but as the saying goes, a true leader "don't think less of themselves, they just think of themselves less."

Or it's what business leader Ken Blanchard calls the difference between a servant leader and a self-serving leader. Very different things indeed and no one wants to be known as a self-serving leader.

Many people assume that leaders always need to be tough and in control. But believe it or not, learning to share the real you with others builds a culture of authenticity and this is perhaps one of the greatest gifts you can give to anyone. The space to be themselves and love them for it.

Leadership is not about changing yourself but developing new skills that inspire, influence and impact. Share your unique self with others, share your personality. Be 100% you and own it.

> *"Great leaders don't set out to be a leader...They set out to make a difference. It's never about the role – always about the goal."*
> **Lisa Haisha**

Humbleness is a self-discovery process. I encourage people to learn about their strengths and weaknesses. As a Gallup Strengths coach, I have found this process incredibly intense and insightful for myself and my team. No one needs to be bulletproof, we're all putting ourselves in positions where we can contribute to society, our workplaces and feel a sense of belonging in doing so.

Back in the day, the old philosophy was that we knew our strengths and weaknesses, and we used to work on our weaknesses to match or control our strengths. Gallup is very different and unique. We encourage people to find their strengths and polish them – make the best of them because you can't be a specialist at everything. So find your strengths and use them. Funny enough, we say that also with our children nowadays, that, "Let's just focus on what you're really great at, and make you absolutely great at it."

Empathy

Another aspect of humbleness is empathy. Empathy is important.

The High-Resolution Leadership report from Development Dimensions International© (DDI), a pioneer in leadership assessment and development for 45 years shows that empathy is the biggest single leadership skill needed today.[12]

The report reveals that leaders who master listening and responding with empathy will perform over 40% higher in overall performance, coaching, engaging others, planning and organising, and decision making. That's one huge statistic. And furthermore, the report is based on the analysis from over 15,000 leaders across 300 companies in 18 countries over 10 years. That's pretty groundbreaking, right?

Richard S. Wellins, Ph.D., Senior Vice President, DDI said, "Being able to listen and respond with empathy is overwhelmingly the one interaction skill that outshines all other skills leaders need to be successful."

And other studies back his assessment. The University of Michigan released a report that showed college students are 40% less likely to have empathy compared to 20 to 30 years ago.[13]

According to the *Wall Street Journal* many employers are now offering 'empathy training' for their employees.[14]

As dentists, empathy should be a strong skill, after all, we are dealing with scared, anxious people every day. However, the flipside is, because

---

12. Development Dimensions International, *The High-Resolution Leadership Report*, www.ddiworld.com/hirezleadership
13. Konrath, Sara H., Edward H. O'Brien, and Courtney Hsing. "Changes in Dispositional Empathy in American College Students Over Time: A Meta-Analysis." Personality and Social Psychology Review 15, no. 2 (May 2011): 180–98. doi:10.1177/1088868310377395.
14. Wall Street Journal, "Companies Try a New Strategy: Empathy Training", Published online June 21, 2016, www.wsj.com/articles/companies-try-a-new-strategy-empathy-1466501403

we deal with so many anxious people, it can become 'the norm' and empathy levels can drop.

It's important as a dentist and a leader that you practise and train in empathy. Like any skill – it can be developed and honed.

Leaders Are 'Why' People

Leadership is also about knowing yourself deeply, developing your strengths and exposing your vulnerabilities.

As I mentioned, I am also trained in Gallup's StrengthsFinder system and I have noticed some themes that run through emerging leaders. They take personal development seriously, they cultivate it, practise it, aim to get better every day.

Often, they have a set of values that they stand by. As the old saying goes, "If you don't stand for something, you'll fall for anything."

I invite you to think about your values and your leadership qualities.

- What do you stand for?

....
....
....
....

- What principles do you refuse to compromise?

....
....
....
....

- What is not up for sale?

....
....
....
....

KNOW YOUR PURPOSE IN THREE MINUTES

Follow this easy equation.

Your PASSION + Your STRENGTHS = Your PURPOSE

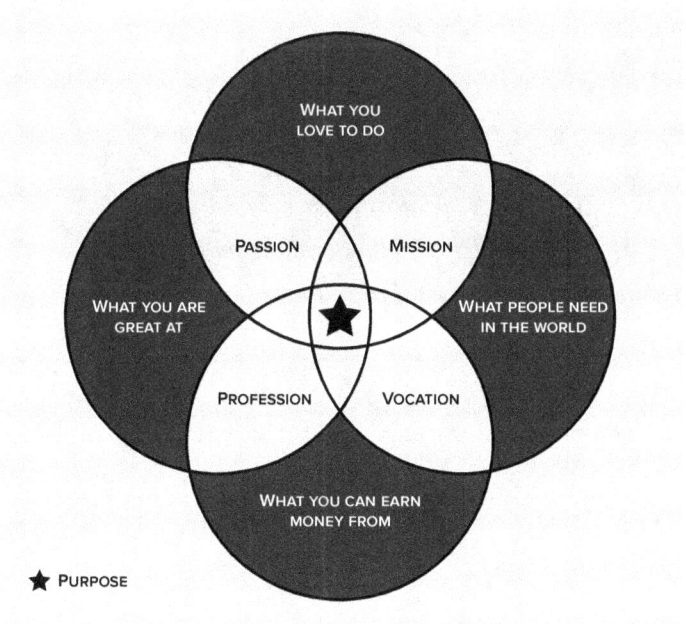

WRITE THESE DOWN:

Strengths

What are your strengths? What are you good at?

....

....

....

....

....

....

....

....

> *"Hide not your talents. They for use were made.*
> *What's a sundial in the shade?"*
> ***Benjamin Franklin***

Passion

What are you most passionate about? What do you love to do?

....

....

....

....

....

....

Humanity
What does the world need?

....

....

....

....

....

Prosperity
What can you be paid for?

....

....

....

....

SOME ADDITIONAL QUESTIONS TO PONDER
What would help you leap out of bed every day with excitement at another day of meaning and adventure?
What is the most important thing in your life?
How does the world need to be changed?
What will you not get bored of?
Where are you helping people?
What have people told you that you're good at?
When have your particular talents been a blessing to people?

RED FLAG ALERTS
Sometimes people do things in order to get something else.

For example, some people get into acting to become famous, not because they love the craft. Or some people become doctors for the money, or follow a career expected of them because their mother or father expected them to do it.

Generally, this doesn't end well.

If you haven't already heard of Simon Sinek's *Know Your Why* book and courses, then I suggest you take a look before you begin.

Here's a basic summary of Sinek's ideas.

Why: This is all about your company purpose. Why your business or company exists. Why you get out of bed every day to go to work and do what you do. It's not about revenue – that the result of what you do, not why you actually do it. The basic premise is – why should people care about you and your company?

How: Perhaps many people and organisations know how they do what they do. They have unique selling points and great marketing strategies. They know HOW they produce their product or service.

What: Now, it's mostly a no-brainer to know what you do. You know what you do in your industry, whether it be manufacturing, marketing or dentistry. You know the service or product you provide. This is your 'what'.

So, taking all this into account – the "Why" is the reason to buy, to care, or to choose. The "Whats" represent the products/service, or the reasons we can say why we like one company over another. The "How" is how companies explain, deliver or market what they do.

Sinek uses Apple as an example of why 'knowing your why' matters. In Sinek's opinion Apple isn't technically different from their competition. But where they do differ is in how they communicate their 'Why'. They show their 'Why'. According to Sinek. Apple's 'Why' is to challenge the status quo and empower the individual. And furthermore, they show their 'Why' through repeated behaviour in everything they do, which is why Apple have built a brand that is perceived as different, authentic and individual. Sinek says that we should all know our 'Why' so we can operate from our true 'Why' and not for other reasons.

2. H – Hungry

Ambitious, Curiosity, Passionate, Innovative, Inspirational

Often influencers have great strengths, but unguarded, these can also be their greatest weakness. Your best can bring you down.

For example, let's look at someone highly-ambitious. Ambition is a great strength that can propel you forward and help you set and achieve goals in incredible amounts of time. Ambition can drive you to find ways to always improve and better yourself. However, some people can be highly ambitious that they become blinded by those around them, they can forfeit important time with family for the sake of work. High ambition can easily slip into being a workaholic.

Imagine two people, Nick and Ken.

Nick is wildly ambitious and pushes and yells for people to get things done.

Ken is equally ambitious but focuses of procedures and productivity, rather than people.

Ken is ambitious, but Nick is blinded by ambition.

Sometimes hunger or ambition is one of those words often preceded by a negative adjective. Your hunger and burning ambition is buried deep within you. Once it is unearthed, you must bridle it like a racehorse to keep it steered in the right direction, in a healthy balance.

Stay hungry and motivated but not arrogant and entitled. Those leaders with a healthy hunger, set new goals and make their entire team healthy.

A great leader is a team player. They hire the right people, put them in the right roles and give them resources they need, and then they get out of their way. Great leaders make everyone around them better.

Develop your character and it will allow you to lead your team, and then build a team culture that helps you thrive your business.

One of the biggest complaints of dental practice owners and many businesses is, "I don't have a great team. My team lets me down. My team is all this – my team is that ..."

They always complain about team problems. But the finger is always pointing to the team, and never at themselves. Sometimes it's okay to point to your team but when you point a finger, don't forget there's four more fingers pointing back at you.

Simon Sinek says, "being a leader is a lifestyle decision; it means you're willing to take care of others."

Yes, leadership is a lifestyle choice. You either make it or you don't. But you can't decide to be a leader when it's convenient. Much like you can't be a parent when it's convenient. You can't be a son or a daughter when it's convenient.

BE THE LEADER

If you want to be a leader – become one.

You can make that decision today.

Begin now to work as though you're in the position of leadership, or the role you want next. Act, lead, dream, dress, create and speak as you would. This requires you to draw new resources from inside yourself. Regardless whether your next goal is to be a small business owner or the Chairperson of an international organisation—think, act, walk, talk and conduct all your affairs as you wish to become.

Experience is what creates expertise. Great leaders do not let mediocrity set in. Push yourself forward on a daily basis.

Every leader must force him/herself to keep learning regardless of his age or stage of life or career.

Well known leader and coach John Wooden said, "A leader who is through learning is through. And so is the team such a leader leads. It's what you learn after you know it all that counts."

I am now more convinced than ever that good leaders develop through constant learning about their personalities and developing their own inner game. They see leadership become better at relationships, communication and caring.

To be a great leader requires you to be INTENTIONAL. Use your hunger in a focused way, an intentional way.

Leaders are readers. I have personally put together a great list of books that made a difference to my life and the way I conduct business. I share them with you at the end of this book as a great resource for developing your leadership capabilities.

3. H – Hustle
Courage, Risk and Action

> *"Good things happen to those who hustle."*
> **Anais Nin**

Hustle means to work hard relentlessly in the face of discomfort to achieve your goals. Being a "hustler" used to once have a negative connotation, and to some it still does. But to me, you can hustle ethically. And you must.

Hustling isn't about taking, it's about doing. It's about getting out there in the world and doing everything you can to make things happen. It's about seeking, discovering and finding opportunities.

Hustlers aren't waiting for the game to be played, they are making the game. Hustlers see the big picture, they are savvy communicators and happy to look beyond the way things have always been done. Hustlers take immediate inspired action.

Hustlers pride themselves in making something out of nothing. They use their talents and resourcefulness to convert their ideas into powerful realities. As Abraham Lincoln said, "Things may come to those who wait, but only the things left by those who hustle."

Hustlers don't wait for success, they go out and make it happen. Being a leader means you tread in new areas and take some calculated risks and immediate action.

Take MIA = Massive Immediate Action and that will make all the difference.

> *"You must either modify your dreams or magnify your skills."*
> *Jim Rohn*

Team Hustle

Leaders are either a hindrance or a genuine asset. You can't half be a half-leader. You're either all in or totally out – you can't do it by halves.

As a dentist, you have to come to the big conclusion that about 80% of your business is run by your team. As dentists get carried away by treating patients, by consulting them and by making and executing treatment plans. The rest is run by a team. Your team is super important to your success.

If your team isn't part of your business hustle, then you'll end up exhausted and burdened. There are some vital elements to providing an efficient and happy workplace, and in the ten strategies that I outline, you will see how important your team really are. In fact, the team hustle is one the most important aspects to your business growth.

The 10 strategies that I outline are so that your team are trained in the MOST effective techniques and correct tools for making team hustle easy and seamless.

To make this all happen, you need to look at these six keys for team hustle:

- Great Team Culture
- High Team Efficiency
- Team Thriving
- Team Joy
- Team Connection
- Investment in Your Leadership

Yes, it's all about TEAM. Don't bypass the need to outline these areas first. A happy and healthy team is critical to your success. And investing in your own leadership skills is critical to their happiness and joy too. The better you can lead, the happier everyone is.

But here's why these simple things are highly successful. Because most people aren't doing them well!

The sad truth is most businesses aren't experiencing much team joy. According to a Gallup report[15], nearly 70% of employees are disengaged at work. And the cost of this lack of engagement is costing organisations billions of dollars per year.

A book called *The 7 Hidden Reasons Employees Leave* by author Leigh Branham, revealed that 89% of bosses believe employees quit their jobs because they want more money. But only 12% of employees actually leave a company for more money.

Yet, Global studies reveal that 79% of people who quit their jobs cite 'lack of appreciation' as their reason for leaving.[16] In other words, people don't leave organisations, or leave for money, they leave because of bosses and managers.

Furthermore, recognition is the number one thing that employees say their boss could give them to inspire them to produce great work. Worldwide studies prove that when it comes to encouraging people to be their best at work, recognition is the most vital. Nothing else comes close — not even higher pay, promotion, autonomy or training.

So recognising your team for a job well done is way more important than you think. And so is trust.

A *Harvard Business Review* survey showed that trust between employee and employer is exceptionally low. 58% of people surveyed said they trust strangers more than their own boss!

Now, that statistic is scary. Or, as I see it, it's an opportunity. It's an opportunity to be different, by building a trusting and supportive network for your team. By appreciating them and understanding that they do about 80% of the work. That they are part of your success team. Your work family.

---

15. 2017, State of the Global Workplace report, Gallup. www.gallup.com
www.gallup.com/workplace/238079/state-global-workplace-2017.aspx
16. Performance Accelerated: A New Benchmark for Initiating Employee Engagement, Retention and Results, www.octanner.com

So being a great leader isn't about your level of charisma, though having some is great too, just don't rely on that for everything. Leadership develops your character. It makes you a better person, not just a better dentist.

"Charisma can run out.
Character shapes you and stays."
Kinnar Shah

COMMUNICATION

What does Adolf Hitler and Martin Luther King Jnr have in common?

Most people assume not much – and they'd be right. Except for one MAJOR thing. They were both world-class communicators. One used communication as a force for good and the other as a force for evil.

But their words inspired action in others. Their words influenced and created impact. They used the art of communication to create world movements – one great for humanity, one that led to destruction.

That's what communication can do. It can make or break people. It can create leaders.

Hitler was very deliberate in mastering the art of public speaking. He wrote all of his speeches himself, sometimes editing them more than five times. He methodically practised his facial expressions and gestures, and used the power of metaphor to influence others.

Martin Luther King Jr.'s drew spiritual inspiration from the Bible, Shakespeare and other civil rights thinkers. He mastered the art of saying what mattered. We all remember the words "not be judged on the colour of their skin, but by the content of their character" and his famous "I Have a Dream" speech.

You see, communication isn't just about what's being said. It's about the action that is inspired from your communication.

And using these two well-known identities show that you can use it as a force for good, or evil.

The fact is this: **being a great communicator is the most important skill you can ever learn.**

There's two types of communication — internal and external.
Internal is how you communicate with yourself
External is how you communicate with others.

INTERNAL COMMUNICATION

There is only one person with whom you communicate 24 hours a day, 7 days a week, 365 days a year. Yourself.

Mastering our self-communication determines our quality of our life.

Communication with yourself includes self-talk or self-thinking. Internal communication is how you run your mind. It's important to know that you run your mind, your mind doesn't run you – unless you let it.

Is it time to become the CEO of your mind? The director of your thoughts?

Understanding the difference between your conscious and subconscious mind is a great first step.

Everybody has a mind but few understand the mechanics of mind.

The conscious mind contains thoughts, memories, feelings, and wishes that we are aware of. These are areas in which we can think and talk about rationally.

The subconscious consists of anything that could potentially be brought into the conscious mind such as memories and stored knowledge.

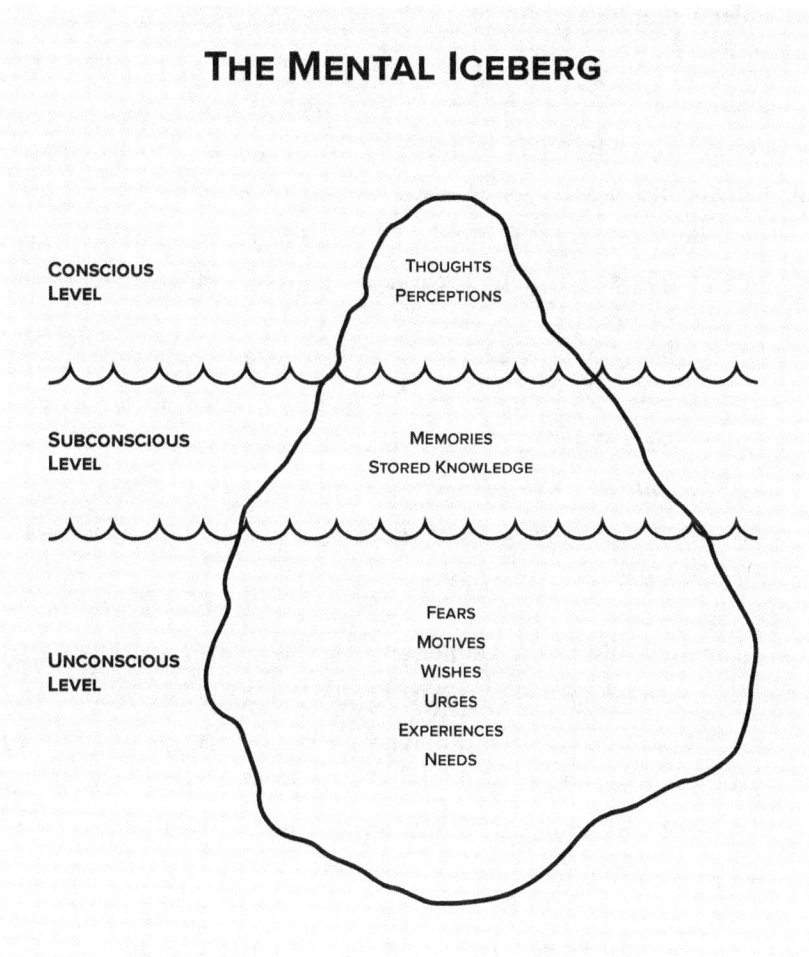

The unconscious mind is a reservoir of beliefs, feelings, thoughts and memories that are outside of our everyday conscious awareness.[17] The unconscious can store some irrational or unacceptable feelings of pain, worry, or conflict. For example, some people fear the dentist from an early childhood experience and this fear stays in the subconscious and gets 'retrieved and believed'.

---

17. Boag S. (2017) Conscious, Preconscious, and Unconscious. In: Zeigler-Hill V., Shackelford T. (eds) Encyclopedia of Personality and Individual Differences. Springer, Cham

Understanding your mind, also helps you understand others. And if you don't take control of your own mind you are essentially allowing the 'programming' to run – whether it's good, bad or indifferent.

Everything you say, believe and do enters the mind – so it's important to be deliberate in what you feed your mind.

The following excerpt is from the Brian Tracy's book *Million Dollar Habits*. It's a simple yet potent reminder about our self-talk.

> *Most psychologists agree that fully 95 percent of your emotions are determined by the things you think and the words you say to yourself as you go through your day. Use your self-discipline and self-control to think and talk about the things you want, rather than allowing your mind to become preoccupied with the things you don't want or that you doubt and fear.*

Muhammad Ali was the king of self-talk. He said, "I am the greatest. I said that even before I knew I was." And we all know his mantra "I am the greatest" became a self-fulfilling prophecy.

If you don't learn how to use your mind, you will allow it to run by default. With the amount of trash being fed to us these days, with social media etc, it's never been more important.

> *"You have power over your mind—not outside events.*
> *Realize this, and you will find strength."*
> *Marcus Aurelius*

THE SUCCESS INGREDIENTS FOR DENTAPRENEURS

Throughout my time coaching and mentoring dental practitioners – I have noticed some regular patterns. Some deeply ingrained patterns that can help or hinder someone's attempt to grow and be greater. These are the ABCDE of Internal Communication. Using them the right way is the ingredients of success.

A – Attitude
B – Beliefs
C – Complaints
D – Day One or One Day?
E – Entitlement

ATTITUDE

Your attitude will dictate your altitude.

Management is what you do, leadership is a mindset and an attitude. Having a bad attitude is like a virus ... it spreads quickly and infects people.

Attitudes are contagious – so infect people with large doses of positivity, joy and good humour. Holocaust survivor, psychiatrist and author of *Man's Search for Meaning,* Viktor E. Frankl said, "Our greatest freedom is the freedom to choose our attitude."

In fact, he believes it can determine who will survive and who won't in uncertain times.

Attitude isn't determined by others, you determine your attitude. But are you deliberate in choosing a good attitude? Even when it's tough? That's the key.

If you think your team lacks passion and enthusiasm, take a hard look in the mirror. Do you lack these qualities? Are they following the leader?

We all like to be around good people, inspirational leaders. Have you noticed that the people who inspire you all have an inspirational attitude? This doesn't happen because they are born with some sort of lucky "good attitude gene" — it's because they developed it, they used it and grew it.

I personally have 5 Attitude Truths that I have lived by every day. These have allowed me to progress rapidly in life and accomplish many of my goals and targets. I'd like to share them with you.

1. There's never any failure, only feedback
2. Communication is your responsibility. You need to check if you have communicated well and people have understood your message. Did the message get through clearly? If not, revise your communication and take responsibility for your part in any miscommunication.
3. Everybody has the resources within to be able to achieve their dreams. Essentially, this means if someone else can do it, then I can do it too.
4. There are no incapable people, only incapable moods or states.
5. The past is not equal to the future. (What got me here won't get me there.)

These have been my North Star when it comes to choosing an attitude and living by it. They have guided many of my decisions and helped me see work and life through a proactive attitude.

> *"Everything can be taken from a man but one thing: the last of the human freedoms — to choose one's attitude in any given set of circumstances, to choose one's own way."*
> **Viktor Frankl**

BELIEFS

As you now know, your brain will act on beliefs. It stores them and acts on what you believe is true. You have to believe that you are capable of achieving and building this dream dental practice by design, and that everything else will fall into place through a series of minor learnings and experiences.

Designing your destiny and not living it by default requires you to run your mind in the most optimal way.

You have empowering and disempowering beliefs, we all do. Your job is to sort through your bunch of beliefs and begin to focus on the beliefs that will get you where you need to go.

Most people are oblivious to the power of their beliefs. Beliefs carry emotion and influence the way we live. Whether you hold negative or positive beliefs about your abilities, your business, your relationships, finances or yourself – they all contribute to the results in your life.

> *"Beliefs have the power to create and the power to destroy. Human beings have the awesome ability to take any experience of their lives and create a meaning that disempowers them or one that can literally save their lives."*
> *Anthony Robbins*

LIMITING BELIEFS

I'm not good enough, smart enough, talented enough to…
I don't have enough money, time, resources
People in business can't be trusted
I can't live my dreams because…
My past is stopping me from success
I'd like to build an empire but I don't think I can

EMPOWERING BELIEFS

I can do anything I put my mind to
People don't limit my success
I am constantly developing and expanding my capabilities
You can teach an old dog new tricks
I am in charge of my life
I am willing and open to live successfully
The best is yet to come

I often suggest to people to take an inventory of their beliefs – to really take a long hard look and see what's going on inside their own mind.

What are you believing about yourself? What do you need to believe about yourself in order to get where you need to go?

Saturate your mind with positive beliefs, infuse your grey matter with affirmations of success, happiness and prosperity.

COMPLAINTS

Are you a complainer? Complainers are a drain to everyone. Do you fall into the trap of complaining and criticising or looking for solutions and results?

Complaining is a habit that some people get stuck in. The glass-half-empty type of people always looking for a problem and never for solutions.

According to Dr. Guy Winch, author of the book *The Squeaky Wheel: Complaining the Right Way to Get Results, Improve Your Relationships, and Enhance Self-Esteem* most people communicate with around an 80% positivity to a 20% negative ratio.

"If it's a 50/50, or you are heavily on the negative side, that's a problem," he says. And the antidote for complainers is to "really look at what matters and what doesn't, because with things that don't matter we need to let go, and the things that matter we have to address."[18]

Complaining can become a really bad habit if you allow it to grow and fester. I suggest you give up complaining, just drop it like you would another bad habit like smoking – go cold turkey and kill off that toxic habit.

Famous American physician and comedic clown, Patch Adams decided to give up bad days all together. He said, "At the age of 18, I made up my mind to never have another bad day in my life. I dove into an endless sea of gratitude from which I've never emerged."

> *"A pessimist is somebody who complains about the noise when opportunity knocks."*

---

18. NBC News Better, Published online, April 26, 2019. By Julie Compton, www.nbcnews.com/better/lifestyle/are-you-chronic-complainer-here-s-how-complaint-cleanse-can-ncna994031

Oscar Wilde

DAY ONE OR ONE DAY?

Are you a 'one day' person? You know the type – *one day* I will begin my own business, *one day* I will earn a decent income. *One day* I will begin my exercise program. *One day* I will go on an overseas trip. But you can pivot this idea immediately by asking yourself this…

Is it One Day or Day One?

You see, you can begin today. You can begin right now. You can make the mental switch immediately and challenge your ingrained psychology to accept the NOW. To take control NOW and begin to make progress, no matter how small in the directions of your dreams.

Be a Day One person. It doesn't matter that it's Day One, it's better than One Day. A million times better. You see, One Day never comes, it's always in the future somewhere. You are always chasing One Day. You never have to chase Day One because it's here and all you have to do is ACT.

> *"Progressive improvement beats delayed perfection."*
> *Mark Twain*

ENTITLEMENT

Some people in positons of influence get a little arrogant and adopt an entitlement mentality, they feel that they are entitled because of their position. When an individual comes to believe that privileges are instead rights, the entitlement mentality is alive and well.

You can't be the victim but you're also not entitled to more privileges than the next person.

Once you think a privilege is a right, you lose a sense of self-determination and if you lose that, you lose a lot.

Millennials and younger generations are often accused of coming to the workplace with a flourishing sense of entitlement. Regardless of age, the only person that is responsible for getting you what you want in life is you. The entitlement mentality of thinking someone owes you something is a short road to small success.

Researchers from Case Western Reserve University found that a sense of entitlement can lead to chronic disappointment because you feel that you deserve certain things and you don't always get them, so you always leave a situation with unmet expectations and disappointment.

I believe this is why many migrants do so well, they come to a new country with very little sense of entitlement. They know it's up to them and they hustle for a great life.

> *"What separates privilege from entitlement is gratitude."*
> **Brené Brown**

EXTERNAL COMMUNICATION

"Who you are speaks so loudly I can't hear what you're saying."
Ralph Waldo Emerson

External is communication with others. It's how you speak, what you say and what you don't say.

MASTER THE 3V'S

The way to do it is to have a mastery or gain mastery of the three Vs, which are: visual communication, vocal communication and verbal communication.

Visual communication is everything to do with body language, vocal communication is everything to do with tone and tenacity and verbal communication is everything to do with the unique language you need to learn to have a higher impact on what you say.

Mastery of the 3 V's makes you successful as it allows you to:

- Inspire
- Influence
- Impact

VISUAL – BODY LANGUAGE

Now let's be honest. A lot of people are scared of dentists, well maybe not dentists but they're scared of going to see a dentist. This includes people of all ages and educational levels. So it won't help your anxious patients if you don't use all the powers of positive persuasion you have to make them feel at ease. Body language is fabulous for this. Because quite often, people won't remember what you say, they'll remember how you made them feel.

Which dentist would you prefer to see?

These ones?

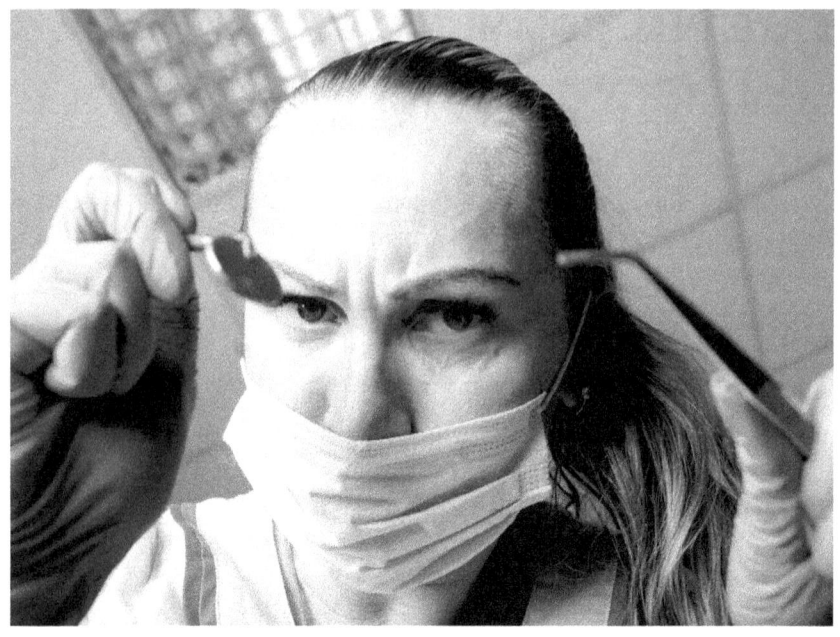

Or these ones?

Obviously, these are extreme image comparisons, but if you think about it. There's no sound, there's no scent, there's no movement other than these still shots. There's only a split second of BODY LANGUAGE.

And that's enough to decide which dentist you like or don't like. One tenth of a second is probably all it took to decide which one you prefer, simply through one still shot of their body.

Now, of course you're not going to be like Steve Martin's insane and sadistic character and dentist, Orin Scrivello, from *Little Shop of Horrors*. But many people find dentists just as scary, so your body language may be exaggerated for them and you have to be very mindful of this. Anxious people can be triggered by small things so displaying warm and confident body language is vital for your business. Even if you have to fake it 'til you make it. Try to be considerate of other people's feelings about your body language. What threatens them may be minor to you but a trigger for them.

Kinesics is the study and interpretation of nonverbal communication related to the movement of our bodies; in other words, it is the study of body language. Science shows that first impressions are made in less than seven seconds and these vital seconds are heavily influenced by your body language. In fact, body language expert Carol Kinsey Goman suggests that nonverbal cues have over four times the impact on the impression you make than anything you say.

The Power of a Handshake

Now you might think the simple handshake doesn't mean much in terms of business success, and I can assure you that's not the case. We use handshakes constantly in our practice and you'll soon find out why.

One study conducted by management experts at the University of Iowa analysed candidate interactions in job interviews and what they found was rather astounding. They discovered that handshakes are "one of the first nonverbal clues we get about the person's overall personality, and that impression is what we remember."

So, yes, people are judging you from the first handshake.

But are you shaking hands?

This is the quickest way to establish rapport. Research shows it takes an average of three hours of continuous interaction to develop the same level of rapport that you can get with one single handshake. But that's not just any handshake by the way, it's a confident and kind handshake (no dead fish, sloppy-style shakes or bone-crushing styles). This is palm-to-palm contact that is firm but not squashing.[19]

New groundbreaking research published in the *Journal of Personality and Social Psychology*,[20] has found that shaking hands can improve the outcome of negotiations for both sides. In fact, it's highly effective to build cooperation and trust. One of the researchers of the study, Juliana Schroeder from the University of California, Berkeley's Haas School of Business says the reason a handshake is so effective is because – "It changes the way you perceive not just the other person, but the way you frame the whole game," she says. "You say to yourself, 'Now we are in a cooperative setting rather than an antagonistic one.'"

And technically she's right. It does in fact suggest cooperation. Archaeology ruins have depicted handshaking practices were used from as far back as ancient Greek times and as early as the 5th Century BC. There are images on ancient pots of people making deals by shaking hands.

I looked into this, and wondered why such a simple thing mattered so much. It seems that back in the times of battles and feuds, many people carried weapons. This could be a sword in a scabbard, which hung around the person's waist, usually on the left. To show the other party that they weren't armed they would extend their right hand out and shake the other person's right hand. This showed that both people came

---

19. https://carolkinseygoman.com
20. Schroeder, Juliana, Jane L. Risen, Francesca Gino, and Michael I. Norton. "Handshaking Promotes Deal-Making by Signalling Cooperative Intent." *Journal of Personality and Social Psychology* 116, no. 5 (May 2019): 743–768.

in peace, that they weren't holding a weapon. Over time, this became a friendly greeting and a sign of trust and safety.

Body Language Speaks More Than You Do

Trust is imperative to a thriving business. Trust is built and established through a congruent alignment between what is being said and the body language that goes with your language. If your gestures aren't congruent with what's being said, people pick this up and subconsciously feel they can't trust you or are uncertain about dealing with you. The reason is there is an internal conflict and they are receiving mixed signals.

Body language expert, Carol Kinsey Goman reported that neuroscientists at Colgate University measured the effects that gestures had on a person's brain by using an electroencephalograph (EEG) machines to measure brain waves activity.[21] When people were shown gestures that contradicted what was being spoken, their brain waves picked up the change. It showed that it had a similar effect on the brain as when people listen to nonsensical language they didn't understand.

So, whenever leaders say one thing and do another with their body language, other people pick it up. Whenever your body language doesn't match your words it sends a signal of distrust. What signs are you sending?

If you don't learn good body language, you're missing half of your business potential.

And if you can't read body language, you are missing half the conversation people are trying to communicate.

Quite often, as a dentist we tend *not* to force clients to over-talk. Who wants to talk with a mouthful of metal, right? So, what you need to remember is that you are talking even when your mouth is shut and their mouth is full of your hands.

Body language is the thing that speaks more than your mouth.

In this fast-paced world of email, texts, webinars and social media,

---

21. Goman, Carol Kinsey, "10 Change Leadership Tips Backed By Science", https://carolkinseygoman.com/10-change-leadership-tips-backed-science

we don't always have a lot of face-to-face contact. But it is the most preferred, productive, and potent communication method we have. And the great news is – you get to use this a lot more than other businesses. In fact, the more business leaders communicate electronically, the more people are wanting more personal interaction. Even in the robotic age, humans still crave a sense of humanity.

Face-to-face communication allows our brains to process all the nonverbal cues we require for building trust, rapport and building professional intimacy. Face-to-face interaction also gives us all the emotional tones behind the words and allows us to communicate care and trust and kindness.

So incredible are the nonverbal bonds between people that when we are in genuine rapport with someone, we unconsciously match our body movements, our breathing rhythms and even our eye-contact frequency with theirs.

These face-to-face meetings trigger our brain's "mirror neurons" which mimic each other's feelings and behaviours. So, a genuine rapport with someone is stronger than you may suspect. We literally impact people from our presence and what we radiate. When we are denied these face-to-face cues, we have no choice but to rely on the printed or spoken word alone, and we need more information to make a decision we feel is right. It takes longer to trust a brochure than it does a genuine person.

As Peter Drucker, a well-known management consultant, said, "The most important thing in communication is hearing what *isn't* said."

Knowing body language helps you see and understand 'engagement signals and behaviours' versus 'non-engagement signals and behaviours'. It helps you become switched-on and savvy to your clients and find solutions for what they want.

Engagement signals indicate agreement and receptivity.
Disengagement signals indicate defensiveness and resistance.

Engagement body signals include:
- Positive head nods or head tilts (like a listening positon)
- Warm smiles
- Open-body positons. When people are engaged, they will usually face you with their whole body.
- Eye-contact. Research shows that most people are comfortable with eye contact that lasts about three seconds, (some cultures less). When we like or feel comfortable with someone this generally increases naturally.

Disengagement body signals include:
- Body positon – when disengaged many people angle their upper body away from you, cross both arms and legs.
- Eye-contact. Disengaged people often look away from you, or at other things and lessen their eye contact time.
- Facial expression – they usually smile less and have tight jaw and more rigid facial expressions.

Facial Expression Patterns

You've probably heard that the new smartphones will all include facial recognition technology. That technology will be able to 'read' your face and identify you. What you may not know is that your brain also has a similar "microchip" that reads faces too. In fact, human beings have been reading faces forever, it's been a natural way to connect, understand and perceive emotions amongst our social interactions and intimate relationships.

I was first introduced to this insightful work through Naomi Tickle's book *You Can Read a Face Like a Book: How Reading Faces Helps You Succeed in Business and Relationships*. As an expert in facial recognition I found that some of her theories paralleled with what I had discovered in practice.

I had discovered that those small miniature (almost unnoticeable) facial expressions often revealed a person's true inner feelings. These mini expressions are now commonly referred to as "micro expressions". Defined as "brief, involuntary facial expression that appears on a person's face according to the emotions being experienced."

Unlike our usual facial expressions, microexpressions are difficult to mask or fake because they are involuntary and ultra-quick. Micro expressions occur in everyone, even without them knowing.

Dr. Paul Ekman, whose groundbreaking research inspired the hit TV show Lie to Me, has shown that facial expressions are a universal language and learning how to read them is trainable to everyone. (www.paulekman.com)

His early research involved clinical cases in which patients lied about their true emotional state. He studied patients who said that they were not depressed and later committed suicide. Upon examining footage of the patients in slow motion, Dr. Ekman and his colleague Dr. Friesen spotted micro facial expressions, which revealed deeper negative feelings the patient was trying to cover-up.

He has spent over a lifetime examining and decoding facial expression for a whole variety of emotions. And the one common denominator is that everyone expresses "facial language" – it's a universal detection device.

In dentistry, learning how to see and notice these microexpressions really helps you understand your clients' true emotions (not the ones they are reporting).

Have you ever heard someone tell you "I'm fine" but the contraction in their pupils held a quick flash of fear? I'm sure you have. It may have only been an instant but you recognised it and knew how they were really feeling. As dentists, we have the advantage of being very close to our patients and seeing their faces, this gives us the scope to be attentive to these microexpressions and tune into our clients.

Scientific findings reveal that even a short amount of exposure (250 milliseconds) provided enough information to correctly identify someone's emotion above the level of "chance".[22]

This incredible skill has been valuable to me in business deals and also talking with staff and networking.

VOCAL – TONE OF VOICE

Your voice is an instrument that can be used in a variety of ways. If you're not using it – you're missing out.

A fascinating study on tone of voice and perception was conducted by The Laboratory of Instrumental Analysis of Communication at the Autonomous University of Barcelona.

Here are some key findings from the research that I'd like to share with you.

- A deeper tone of voice is considered more mature and generates feelings of trust in others. It is also the chosen tone range for radio hosts and advertising voice overs.
- An extremely deep voice can convey a dark feeling in the listeners.
- A firm yet confident vocal style can portray the talker as important and more distinguished.
- A voice that is very quiet can make the listener believe that the talker is a little awkward or has some major weaknesses.
- People that have a high-pitched voice can come across as immature and can often seem to lack credibility.

Changes in the use of voice are clearly perceived by the listeners, we pick these things up subconsciously and consciously and make judgements and decisions around them.

Your voice is exceptionally personal and it's becoming a very unique business tool to use.

---

22. Laura Martinez, Virginia B. Falvello, Hillel Aviezer & Alexander Todorov (2016) Contributions of facial expressions and body language to the rapid perception of dynamic emotions, Cognition and Emotion, 30:5, 939-952, DOI: 10.1080/02699931.2015.1035229

But a new study by Michael Kraus of the Yale University School of Management has shown that hearing is vital when it comes to accurately detecting emotion.[23] Kraus found that we are more accurate when we hear someone's voice than when we only look at their facial expressions. Kraus also found that this is true even when we see their face and hear their voice. This means, you may be able to sense someone's emotional mood even better over the phone than in person. So even the way your dental practice answers the telephone is important (we will discuss this at length in the 10 Strategies section).

Even the speed at which you communicate matters. Too slow can come across as lacking interest, too fast can increase stress and tension.

Tone of voice is a tool we use every day. When we want to convey excitement – we naturally raise our voice and when we get serous – we tend to lower our voice. When a heated argument may arise, to calm someone down we tend to use a slower, easier tone to increase calm and clarity.

VERBAL

What you say matters. Words have the ability to heal, hurt and hinder. Use them wisely.

Words aren't a series of letters in the alphabet all sewn together, they are cues, triggers, bridges that form bonds, sequences that impact, influence and persuade.

Ethical persuasive language, NLP, Hypnotic language patterns

Ethical persuasion techniques allows you to lead and motivate your team, and helps patients accept and act on your recommendations.

Words when used correctly can convert "I'm scared" into "I'm happy to go ahead with my new dental plan." Or "I can't get through my business plateau" to "I am ready to innovate."

---

23. Kraus, Michael W., *Voice-Only Communication Enhances Empathic Accuracy*, Yale University, School of Management.

Words can take you from "no" to "let's go" – if you know how to use them.

A recent study at Stanford University[24] showed that kind and encouraging words from a doctor reduced the recovery time of patients.

According to authors Andrew Newberg, M.D. and Mark Roberts Waldman, in their book, *Words Can Change Your Brain*, even "a single word has the power to influence the expression of genes that regulate physical and emotional stress."

This means words change our brains, bodies and feelings. They wrote:

"By holding a positive and optimistic [word] in your mind, you stimulate frontal lobe activity. This area includes specific language centers that connect directly to the motor cortex responsible for moving you into action.
And as our research has shown, the longer you concentrate on positive words, the more you begin to affect other areas of the brain. Functions in the parietal lobe start to change, which changes your perception of yourself and the people you interact with."

They also suggest that the rate of your speech influences how the other person feels, and that using your body language well conveys more meaning than words can capture.

Now, these just aren't opinions, these experts showed the power of words via brain scans and from their studies, they believe that we can all develop and use these tools by practicing some simple strategies for a few minutes a day. And the results can lead to great outcomes for you and the people you interact with.

In my workshops, we go through these ideas and role-play them. We ensure that the words used are ethical and effective. That they land and have meaning.

---

24. 20 August 2018, Leibowitz, K.A., Hardebeck, E.J., Goyer, J.P. et al. J GEN INTERN MED (2018) 33: 2051, https://doi.org/10.1007/s11606-018-4627-z

Words are highly emotional things for us humans. Think of how powerful these three words are:

I love you
I hate you
Go for it!
What's the price?
What's your secret?
Who's your mentor?
Who's your dentist?

It's the underlying emotion that drives that action. If you *feel* emotion, you take action. But as humans we also like meaning and reason.

In the book *Influence* by Robert Cialdini, one study showed different phrases that were tested to see which one would make people more inclined to allow someone to break in line at the copy machine.

- "Excuse me, I have 5 pages. May I use the Xerox machine?" – **60%** allowed the person to cut in line.
- "I have 5 pages. May I use the Xerox machine, *because* I am in a rush?" – **94%** allowed the person to cut in line.
- "Excuse me, I have 5 pages. May I use the Xerox machine *because* I have to make copies?" – **93%** allowed the person to cut in line.

Simply hearing a "because" followed by a reason, meant that nearly every person could get in front of them in line. The reasons given weren't even detailed.

But the takeaway here is that humans love to know why. We need to know why. Why do you need that dental work done soon? Because it will help you...

Verbal Commitment

Getting verbal commitment is also a great way to use your voice. When someone gives a verbal commitment it increases compliance, and we know how important compliance is in the dental industry, don't we? It's essential. We need patients to cooperate and comply with our recommendations.

A study[25] published in the *Journal of Applied Social Psychology* conducted two experiments to see if blood donor attendance could be increased by altering the content of reminder calls. The blood donor organisation increased participation from 70% to 82.4% simply by changing their wording from "We'll mark you on the list as coming then, thank you" to "We'll mark you on the list as coming then, okay? [Pause for confirmation]. Thank you."

Verbal commitment increased attendance. And it was the confirmation that changed the game.

Knowing the right questions, using the right language is important to make people feel safe and getting them to feel compliant not resistant.

The One Word People Google A Lot

How many times have you searched something on the internet and put the word "best" in front of your search. The *best* business books, the *best* way to build a dental practice, the *best* accommodation in Sydney, the *best* restaurant in Melbourne.

Think about it, which sounds better? "How to clean your teeth" *or* "The best way to clean your teeth."?

"See the dentist" or "See the best dentist." Which one has more influence?

Using the word best implies there's a comparison, and you come out on top. But remember calling yourself the 'best' is not just a word to use, you actually have to be the best at something. Maybe you're the best dentist in town, or the best at veneers or the best service, or the best at treating people with respect and care. Find your best and be it!

---

25. Lipsitz, A. , Kallmeyer, K. , Ferguson, M. and Abas, A. (1989), Counting On Blood Donors: Increasing the Impact of Reminder Calls. Journal of Applied Social Psychology, 19: 1057-1067. doi:10.1111/j.1559-1816.1989.tb01239.x

10 Things Great Leaders Never Say...
1. I think
2. I'll try
3. Don't bring me bad news or surprises
4. You're just lucky to have a job
5. I'm the boss, you're the employee
6. That's not my fault
7. Failure is not an option
8. I had great results this year
9. I like people who think like me
10. I hate my job

10 Things Great Leaders Say...
1. We did it!
2. Well done
3. How can I best support you?
4. What do you think?
5. I have trust in you
6. "Thank you" and "Please"
7. What's the best way for us?
8. I appreciate you and your contribution
9. We are a great team
10. How can we improve?

The Body Language of Great Leaders
- Leaders walk with a healthy confidence
- They send congruent nonverbal signals of warmth and empathy
- They make eye contact with lots of people (not just the most important person in the room)
- They have mastered the genuine handshake and use it often
- They look for the body language cues of others and adapt to situations

- They use open body positons and congruent gestures
- They smile often
- They notice microexpressions

The Communication of Great Leaders
- They use positive life-affirming words
- They mean what they say and say what they mean
- They use people's names
- They are congruent and clear communicators
- Their words match their body language

COMMUNICATION IS THE #1 SKILL IN THE WORLD

Again, these skills weren't taught to me at university, they were the ones I sought out and found myself. But these were the skills that made all the difference to the way I saw my role as a dentist and my role in creating my own destiny.

I've spent over 12 years studying visual, verbal and vocal communication. It's something that I have spent thousands of hours practising in order to achieve a level of mastery. And that's why I am now teaching others these skills — because they were vital to my success. I want others to know the secret weapon, to take advantage of this incredibly powerful skillset and watch their lives and their businesses explode to a new level.

But it's not just me advocating for this now, research is now revealing the very same conclusions as those who have been in the 'business trenches' learning through trial and error.

Professor Colin McLeod – Program Director, Master of Entrepreneurship in the Faculty of Business and Economics at University of Melbourne wrote:

'We are seeing record numbers of business graduates from universities around the world, at the same time as higher numbers of entrepreneurs' report failure to grow or even survive. A lack of marketing, finance and business management skills is frequently associated with start-up failure in Australia and overseas. It seems entrepreneurs either do not have the opportunity to acquire these skills for themselves or lack the networks and expertise to attract these vital skills to their business.' [26]

He's right. That was my story too. But it's not too late to learn these new skills. It's never too late to learn how to lead, how to run a booming business and how to communicate effectively.

---

26. Professor Colin McLeod – Program Director, Master of Entrepreneurship in the Faculty of Business and Economics at University of Melbourne, Pursuit, WHY ARE AUSTRALIAN START-UPS FAILING?, https://pursuit.unimelb.edu.au/articles/why-are-australian-start-ups-failing

I ask all Dentapreneurs to take this skill seriously, just like you have acquired your dental education; because the truth is – this is a large portion of your business. It's a large part of life.

I'm going to stress this point again because if you miss it, you'll miss the success it brings you too. **The number #1 skill all Dentapreneurs should have is effective communication.**

If you don't know where to start, then let me help. This is not to sound like a blatant sales gimmick – I mean everything I say. To maximise your business growth, you can't leave yourself out of the equation. You are the cog of the wheel that spins the success. You need to maximise your ability to influence, inspire and impact.

If you're ready to grow and develop your natural leadership tendencies – then come to one of my programs and begin now. You will never regret building the #1 business skill in the world. And even if you don't think you're ready, then you *really* need to be there, because what you will learn may in fact change your thinking forever. If you don't come out of one of my workshops or events with a life-changing skill that you can use for the rest of your life, then shame on me. I'll even hand back your money. But that won't happen because I can guarantee you will get a life-changing skill. Let me explain how I know this for sure.

Could you imagine someone telling you that you don't know how to complete a dental filling? Imagine that. You're a practising professional dentist and someone has the audacity to say you don't even know how to complete a dental filling. You'd laugh, right? Because you know you can do fillings in your sleep. And so you should – you studied for years and years. You did the theory, you did the practice, you give people fillings every day. That's why you're a professional.

Now, to someone who doesn't know much about fillings – what could you teach them about fillings in two days? You give them a complete 180-degree change. They'd go from not knowing much to knowing quite a bit.

Now, I've been studying the art of influential communication for over 12 solid years. Obsessively! I know the theory, sure — but more importantly I have used it continually and practically in my own dental practice all this time. I use it in business, in life and couldn't have any degree of success that I've had without this skill.

Now, imagine that all the best things from my 12 years of study got condensed down into only the very best. That within only two days you received the best of my 12 years' knowledge and received only the most highly-effective skills that rapidly changed my business and can rapidly change yours. Would that sound like well-spent time?

Well, it is. Essentially that's what everything I do is all about. Highly effective, tried-and-tested strategies that I can guarantee work if you implement them.

For more information, or to register go to: **kinnarshah.com/events**

PART 2

IS KINNAR CRAZY?

So, when I tell fellow dentists that they can have a million-dollar *per chair* practice, some look at me suspiciously. Some new dentists think I've lost my mind.

Let me assure you, I'm not into wasting people's time or offering bullshit for sale. I'm not saying that building my first millon-dollar per chair practice was easy, but it wasn't hard either. And I'm no snake-oil salesman. I'm telling you this because it's true. It's not about the money, it's about what's possible. It's not crazy to believe you can have a number of 1.5 million-dollar chairs per year in your practice.

I was born and raised in Mombasa city in Kenya, Africa. The first 18 years of my life were spent there. We weren't rich but we weren't poor. We were average. Mum and Dad always made sure that we had food on the table and clothes on our body. They also made sure we were educated.

Now, most people know three things about Kenya – we have supreme marathon runners, exotic safaris and *Hakuna Matata*.

You say 'Hakuna Matata' and most people know the song from *The Lion King* and start singing. In Kenya, it's our version of "no worries."

The term 'no worries' is also used as a great mantra by many Aussies, so when I came here, it was great to know the "no worries" philosophy was universally accepted. Hakuna Matata is a great term for us dentists because we deal with so many anxious people all the time, but I like to use it in more of a broad sense. I use Hakuna Matata in business, not in a way to turn a blind-eye and say yeah, no worries. But to know if you're working hard and doing all the right things, then everything will fall into place and you won't have to waste a moment in worry. Hakuna Matata!

From my beloved Kenya, I travelled to the United Kingdom University of Glasgow where I studied dentistry. Now dentistry wasn't totally easy for me, in fact, I was in the bottom 20% of my class. I had to really hustle my butt to graduate, and I did. All I really wanted to do was just pass the exams because even back then I could intrinsically sense an unnamed disconnect between what I was learning and how to apply it to the real world. It was like a nagging gap that lingered in the background of my thinking but I was unable to join the dots.

After I graduated, I came to Sydney, Australia, and have been here ever since. For the first three years of my work as a dentist here, I was an associate dentist. I took this role seriously and applied myself vigorously to developing my clinical skills. I was so motivated to be the best dentist I could that I spent around 50 cents of every dollar I earned on developing more advanced clinical skills. I did this with full unbridled gusto for three years straight.

Until, one unsuspecting day, it dawned on me. Despite my advanced clinical skills and my supercharged levels of motivation – I was not experiencing economic growth. Something wasn't adding up. How could I be getting better but not richer? How could I be working harder but not getting ahead?

This is not uncommon for dentists. It can be quite baffling. When I ask other dental owners' what stands between them and their dreams, most say things like fear, lack of staff, more time, more money.

They're all great and worthy answers, but they're not the essential thing.

The transition from being an associate dentist to being a business owner was a life-changing moment for me. It showed me the price of my dreams. It gave me a vision of business that I had never had before.

In the first three years of being an associate dentist in Sydney, I was working for a dentist owner called Rob. Rob was a great guy, and even though I had my own dreams of running my own dental practice, I was happy to have a job.

After a couple of years of working for Rob, one day, I went to him and politely said, "Rob, I've been working for you for a couple of years now and I want to become an entrepreneur, I want to open my own dental practice, it's been my dream for quite some time."

Rob looked at me and said, "Really, Kinnar? That's an amazing dream. But you can't leave."

I looked back at Rob and said, "What do you mean I can't leave?"

He said, "Well, Kinnar, I've been thinking about this. You've been working for me for two years now and you've been great. How about if I were to raise your salary?"

I looked back at Rob and said, "Rob, that is an amazing offer but this is my dream and I really want to pursue it, I just want to open my own practice."

Rob looked back, "Kinnar" he said. "I understand and I think it's great. But what if I were to raise your salary up another 10%?"

I said, "Rob, I appreciate that you're raising my salary but this is not a financial decision. This is a dream decision for me. I really want to open my own practice."

Rob frowned. "Kinnar, believe me, I really appreciate what you're saying and I understand where you're coming from. Well…what if I were to raise your salary again?"

Now, I kid you not. This is a true story. I was gobsmacked by this stage. In fact, even though I kept saying 'no' — Rob offered to raise my salary four times throughout our conversation.

Until Rob finally said, "Kinnar, all right, okay. Listen – you drive a hard bargain. What if I were to raise your salary more than six figures, I want to give you over $100,000?"

Now, ladies and gentlemen, this is going back about 16 years ago. $100,000 was a lot of money back then. It's a lot of money right now. I wasn't earning money like that back then.

I looked at Rob and I said, "Rob, dreams are overrated." We had a laugh.

I thought of my wife and said, "Rob, it's all good but you know, I need to go on and discuss this with my wife." (The husbands' reading this book will understand the need to do this, won't you?)

So I went back home. I said, "Honey, I don't know what to do. What should I do?"

My wife was cooking a curry in the kitchen. She looked up at me with her big, brown eyes and she said, "Take the money, fool!"

Now, most of you are probably thinking that my wife is both smart and savvy. Which she is. But then she stopped cooking the curry and called me to sit on our beaten up, old black, leather sofa. She looked at me sincerely and said, "Kinnar, for the last nine months, all you've been talking about is how you want to open your own practice, how you want to live your dream practice. I don't care how much money he gives you. Go back and tell him that *Your Dream is Not for Sale*."

Now that sentence changed the course of my life. That comment pivoted me to see dreams as priceless. That sentence gave me the courage to tell Rob my dream didn't have a price-tag attached to it.

I have now been a dental practice owner for 15 years. My brothers, Dr Manish Shah (also a dentist) and Business Manager, Vikit Shah are also part of the business. Together, we support each other to grow and develop both as individuals and also as a business.

GOOD IS A STEPPING STONE

Most people have a dream, many even pursue them — if they don't have to risk a lot. A regular dream has a dollar-value. A real dream is priceless. And how to tell the difference between a standard dream and a real dream is that the real dream won't go away.

Even if I took that offer from Rob, sure I may have been richer in the short-term, but I would have been poorer both emotionally and financially in the long-term. My wife was right, some dreams just aren't for sale.

The number one thing that stands between most people in achieving their true dreams is something good they settle for. Most people settle for good. Most dentists I know settle for good. Good marketing systems, good team, good telephone technique, good conversion rates, good income.

Good is just that – it's good.

But why can't you make a decision to go for great?

You see good is a mindset pattern. We settle. We feel satisfied. We don't go further because we feel content. Content is lovely, but great is exhilarating. Great is challenging. Great lights a fire within and gets the juices of life flowing. Great trumps good every time.

Like the research earlier, 68% of the successful dentists didn't have a plan for their future. In other words, they didn't have a plan to go from good to great.

The first thing I encourage "good businesses" to do is to stop settling for mediocre. To make a firm commitment and a decision to yourself, to your team and your family, that you're going to go for great.

And if you haven't made this decision yet, then I suggest you do because everything that I'm about to share with you depends on you making this decision. Being willing to transform from good to great.

But let me also say, it's important to acknowledge where you are already. You have obtained some degree of success already. So that's awesome. But it's important to understand that what has got you here, won't be the same as what takes you higher. You need to keep improving if you want to go up the ladder of life and obtain different results.

As Einstein said, "Problems cannot be solved with the same mindset that created them."

Much like a new level of great, cannot be created if you only use "good" strategies.

If you are dedicated to success, then you must adopt a great mindset, great strategies and do it with great zest and enthusiasm.

You see, when I first started running my own business practice, I didn't have any mentors. I didn't know that dentistry wasn't about teeth. I didn't know that a good business wasn't a great business.

And just like any new business owner, I ran into a marvellous collection of problems. Without any face-to-face mentors, I realised that what I needed wasn't another technical dental course, I needed a business course. I needed to hone and sharpen my people skills and learn advanced communication techniques.

It hit me like a sledge-hammer to the head. Like a cannonball to the guts. The epiphany struck. I felt baffled. Why hadn't I seen this before? It was all so obvious.

But like most dentists, I was so gung-ho on being an excellent dentist, I didn't focus on running an excellent business. That is, until I did. And the results of that epiphany and the action from the realisation is the very reason why I am here writing this book today.

Without these two moments, my life could have been vastly different and I may not have had the success I have today:

1. The moment my wife said, "your dream is not for sale"
2. And the moment I had the epiphany that dental school only prepared me for the very basics, and I had to invest heavily not only on further clinical education, but most importantly on business, leadership and communication skills to build a viable and thriving dental practice so I could help and serve even more patients.

The reason I have decided to share all my hard-earned strategies and secrets to success in this book is because I have been that dentist without a mentor. I have been that dentist starting a business and wanting to grow it.

I started my business from scratch after a few years in a new country. I really just want to say to others, "If I can do it, so can you."

In reflection, I can see that three things were vital, three inner traits that without them, I certainly not would be where I am today. They are: **patience, potential** and **persistence**.

Life certainly gives us a lesson in all three areas. We must have patience, patience allows us to know that the seeds we plant today will harvest in the future. We must cultivate our vision to see and believe in our own potential and the potential of others. We must have persistence to keep going despite the obstacles.

Over the last six years through seminars, workshops and webinars, I've been helping hundreds and hundreds of dental owners understand what is required to build a great business.

Now, I am going to share the blueprint and all the executive steps with you to achieve this. But there's one thing I can't do for you – I can't make the decision for you. I can give you all the tools you'll need, but I can't switch your brain into saying "yes to success". That part is your job. Your contribution.

I ask you to take a minute to really think about it. Think about what absolutely needs to be done in your business to make it great.

To think deeper about this, let's look at some figures. Some good businesses make around $300-$600K per chair. Of course, it's not about the chair. The chair is how many patients feel happy and confident to get their dental work done in your business.

It's a very intimate and anxious thing for many people. So if you're getting bums on seats, you're doing more than just filling seats. You're making people feel more comfortable than your competitor.

A great chair is about 1.2 – 1.5 million dollars. Some great businesses have up to five of these chairs and are servicing their clients and team in a powerful way.

I am a serial entrepreneur, but at the end of the day, the truth is, that I just love helping other people grow. I'm obsessed with it. I love the human brain, I love connecting us all. I love knowing that we can each have a level of success beyond our wildest dreams.

And the only reason I know this is because I took the journey. I walked the path with my own two shoes and now I want others along for the wild ride. It thrills me.

I tell people to only listen to those who have the success you want. Don't listen to all the naysayers and victims and complainers that mope around telling you why you can't "make it". That's bullshit. YOU CAN!

I'm living proof. Anthony Robbins says, "If you want to be successful, find someone who has achieved the results you want and copy what they do and you'll achieve the same results."

I agree. Actively seek out the people who have achieved success ask them what have they done and do it. Just make sure it's actual success, not the appearance of success.

For me, those people and mentors were authors. Business leaders and influencers who shared knowledge and gave me their wisdom. I have decided to become one, to use the power of books too. To give back to those who may not have a mentor they can call on or someone they know who built a thriving dental practice.

Too many people like to tell you why you can't do something. This book isn't for them. Complainers and critics will always look at achievers and call it "luck". But you and I both know that fortune favours the brave. Fortune favours the ones who have a plan. A roadmap of how to get you where you want to go.

This my fellow Dentapreneurs, this is your ultimate blueprint. Your roadmap to GREATNESS. That is, if you made the decision to be great? Did you? If you didn't, this book is not for you.

YOUR DENTAL PRACTICE BLUEPRINT

The funny thing about business is that quite often you need to make decisions like you're already a billionaire, even if you're not. Now, why would I say something so bold? How could you make a billion-dollar decision if you've never been a billionaire? How would you even know what a billionaire decision is?

So let me save you the pondering. Let me give you the punchline right upfront.

The only thing a billionaire and a beggar have in common is *time*. Despite their economic polarity they each have 24 hours in a day and 7 days a week.

The billionaire has exactly the same amount of time as the beggar, they have just used it differently.

How people spend their time determines their outcomes. A billionaire uses their time in a way that compounds their dollars without stealing from their time.

So, let's keep this simple and think in terms of business time. Imagine you spend five days a week working. What are you actually doing in that time? What are your team doing? Are you spending that time doing things that compound your money and reduce your time? Or are you running around like a headless chook trying to do everything and not getting anything accomplished?

You see, I see a lot of dental practice owners and their teams spend their valuable time and energy in "fluff duties" – stuff that doesn't really make the business thrive. Sure, some "fluff duties" may be necessary but they're not where you should be focusing your time.

And that's what we're going to be looking at in this chapter. I am going to reveal what you need to focus on in order to exponentially grow your practice. And it is a NEED, not a WANT.

If you want to skyrocket to the next level – it's not all about your wants — it's about what you NEED to do, what you MUST do if you want to get there.

And when you get there – you'll get what you want, which is more time, money, freedom – right?

So, let's look at how you currently use your time.

Where is your and your team's time spent the most? Don't skip ahead, just take a pen and write down where you and your team currently spend your time. I'll explain why after.

1. _____
2. _____
3. _____
4. _____
5. _____
6. _____
7. _____
8. _____
9. _____
10. _____

THE ONE RULE THAT WILL RADICALLY CHANGE YOUR BUSINESS FOREVER

Now, have you ever heard of The Pareto Principle? Or what is commonly known as the 80/20 rule? It was named after Italian economist Vilfredo Pareto who realised that 80% of consequences come from 20% of the causes. In fact, his original observation concluded that 80% of Italy's wealth belonged to only 20% of the population.

Regardless of whether it is scales of economy or time, the Pareto Principle basically indicates that there's an unequal balance between inputs and outputs. For example, 20% of a company's staff could drive 80% of the company profit.

The Pareto Principle can be applied especially to businesses that are client or service-based, like dentistry. Though, don't take the mathematics as a "law" or an "equation", it's an overall observation. The main take away is this:

Look at what you do and what it gives you – so you know what to focus on and what to delegate or give up.

Let's get specific, if 20% of your customers contribute 80% of your business results: focus on rewarding those customers for their loyalty and attracting new ones. You can't rely solely on your 20% but YOU MUST look after your 80% revenue FIRST.

Don't give up your loyal customers giving you 80% of your turnover in the vain attempt to get new ones. Look after them first, and also grow with new clients.

If 20% of your staff contribute to 80% of your problems: focus on training your staff and getting those problems fixed immediately.

If 80% of your time is taken up for 20% of your profit: re-evaluate how you spend your time.

Get the idea?

You must apply this principle directly to your time and your business to succeed.

So, your list may consist of many things. After all, running a business means that every day multiple things get thrown at you to deal with.

One of my favourite books *Sell Like Crazy* by Sabri Suby, CEO of Australia's fastest growing direct marketing agency, King Kong, outlines the Pareto Principle rule better than anyone. He points out the same red flag as I'm saying here. He calls them 'little chores'. Describing them as 'things that keep you busy but don't make you any money... or even worse, lose you money.' He says to focus on the activities that produce the bulk of your revenue. What he refers to as Highly Leveraged Activities.

I agree. This principle turned my business and my time-management around in seconds. I simply listed all the activities I could get someone else to do, 'the little chores', and focused on what produced the highest yielding results. This didn't mean charging clients more, it meant what made my business operate better, what produced results.

After all, isn't it wonderful to give more dentists a job in your business? Help your staff have a great income and happy workplace? Isn't it great to have a happy, healthy business for your clients, your staff and your family?

So, I went rogue and deleted or delegated those things I didn't need to do. I sat down and figured out where my time was best spent. What made the business prosperous? What makes it good?

I didn't just focus on business. What were the other things I could get someone else to do so I could focus on what was the MOST important aspect of the business?

I hired someone to do all my admin and accounts. I stopped cleaning my car and paid someone to do it. After all, what I paid someone for one hour, actually saved me an hour of my income. Which meant, I saved money by paying them.

My to-do list got shorter but more potent. I was ONLY focusing on those **high-return activities**.

And it's these high-return activities that completely transformed my business and life. And I am going to give you the best 10 strategies in this book. You will be given the 10 high-yielding strategies of success so you can stay in the lane of prosperity and freedom and never return back.

In a nutshell, here's what I did.

I focused on what brought me 80% results from 20% of my time.

Simple. In other words, I focused on high yielding important tasks that drove business success and brought in 80% of the results and stopped filling my time with all the "fluff activities" that gave me only 20% results.

So as you can see the change in balance and scaling your time, revenue and effectiveness, then looks more like this:

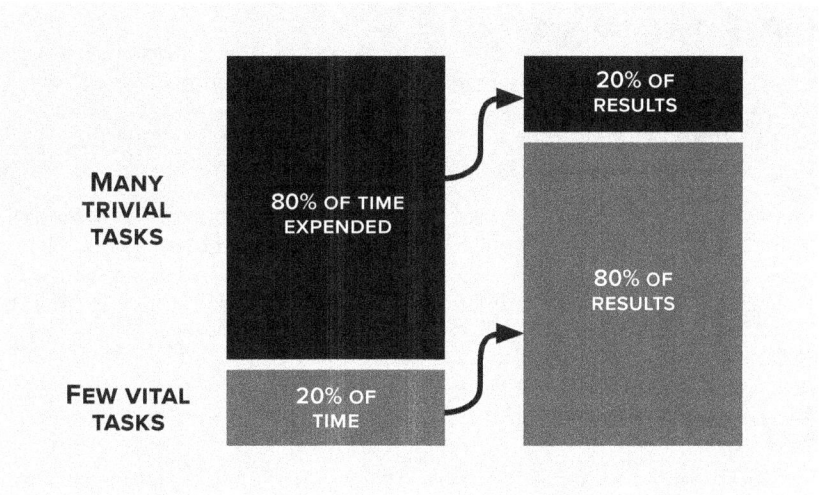

The old adage "Time is money" is true. You may have eight working hours a day. Your staff have eight working hours a day. But what you're doing with those hours determines your level of success. Those eight hours can be focused on high yielding activities or they can be focused on running around trying to do everything all at once.

Now the 10 strategies I will be giving you are in fact more important than the systems.

To make this clear, let me give you my definition of a strategy and a system.

A strategy = a system done in a unique way.

A system = what everyone needs to implement.

For example, how to switch a computer on is a system. There's no unique way of switching on a computer. But if I tell you how to give customer service, that's a strategy. There's a unique way to do it.

Strategies set you apart from the crowd. You don't have the herd mentality. Systems are part of the everyday running of a business.

Therefore, a strategy is the most important focus because it includes a system done in a unique way.

LEVERAGING TIME

One of biggest advantages to using these 10 strategies in businesses is leveraging time.

Leveraging time is getting other people to multiply your time, which means having 100-hours of work per day rather than eight-hours a day.

Most people do systems rather than strategies.

For example, a typical old system for introducing a new patient into your practice for the first time could be an 'Introductory strategy' like this: "Good morning Mrs Jones. Please have a seat. The doctor will be with you in a minute."

Others use a strategy – "Good morning Mrs Jones, welcome to Smile Concepts," shake hands – "My name is Silvia and I will be looking after you today."

That's a strategy. It's a system done is a unique and effective way.

Many dental practices are currently marketing themselves to the public like a system. But how can you be unique? Marketing is a system, marketing your company in a unique way to enhance your unique selling points is a strategy.

These 10 strategies will start you thinking and implementing new ways to set yourself apart and exponentially grow your practice.

And you need to be unique and different because often the biggest challenges facing dentists is competition. Competition rises. So you need a catchy way to stand above the rest.

Now, there are two kinds of people out there, those who criticise and complain and those who go and get results. And in our dental industry, more people are giving excuses than getting results. My challenge to you is: give up criticising and complaining and start trying these new strategies. Begin to grow today, not tomorrow.

Seize the day!

Kinnar is sharing more in his INTERACTIVE book.

See exclusive, behind-the-scenes videos, audios and photos.

DOWNLOAD free content and learn how to exponentially grow your dental practice.

deanpublishing.com/dentapreneur

FOUR STAGES OF A DENTAL BUSINESS

As a dental practice owner, you must know that its normal for a practice to go through four main stages. Throughout each stage you will encounter different challenges. For a business to really boom it takes some time to mature and grow, but it certainly doesn't take forever.

As you go along your Dentapreneur journey, you will certainly encounter different stages of growth, but see each stage as a stepping stone to greatness, because that's exactly what it is.

Start-up Stage

Period: 1 – 2 years
Important marker: To break even in terms of expenses versus income.

The survival stage is the stage where a dental practitioner has just purchased a business. Naturally, this stage involves the cost to buy a practice, the equipment and the goodwill to take on business. It's the stage where you are trying to make ends-meet and just getting used to the new environment and the new stage of your business journey.

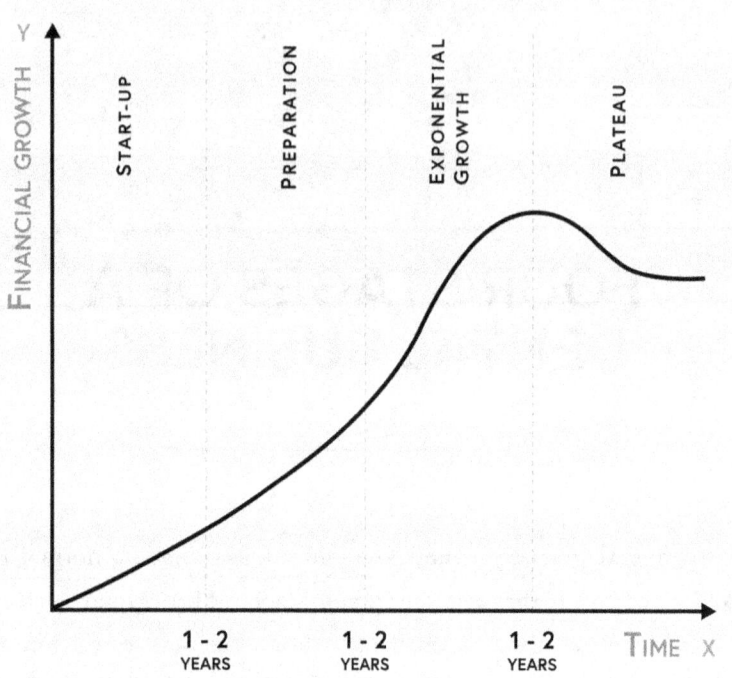

You get to know the internal and external environment more. You learn about your location and its demographic in a more intimate way, you begin to meet local people and local businesses. You begin to understand the demands of business and the unique situation of hiring staff and managing clients.

The important marker for this stage is for you to be breaking even in terms of expenses versus income. Now, the Start-up Stage isn't supposed to be a long-term situation. It's really just to find your feet and graduate to being a business owner.

Now, when dentists surpass the Start-up Stage, they graduate to something called the Preparation Stage.

Preparation Stage

Period: 1-2 years

Important Marker: Focusing on correct systems and strategies.

Once you have surpassed the Start-up Stage, you graduate into a new phase of your business, this is the time when you've put your strategies and systems in place. Now, this stage is critical because I have seen many many dentists remain stuck in this stage. The Preparation Stage should really be a stepping stone in your business, a place for you to launch into massive growth. Yet, I have coached and consulted hundreds of dentists who discovered they were stuck here. And by stuck, I mean well and truly stuck in the Preparation Stage for more than five to ten years.

This Preparation Stage should not take more than another one to two years. So, why do people get stuck here? Because they don't know which systems and strategies to focus on. There are over 50 systems in a dental practice. And here's the major thing most dental practitioners don't know:

Out of those 50 systems, only 10 bring you 80% of your revenue.

So the reason, businesses get stuck here is because they don't know which 10 to focus on. They attempt to focus on all 50 and end up spinning around on the hamster wheel and never obtain exponential business growth. Many are stuck here because they're not focusing their time in the right direction.

Exponential Growth Stage

Period: Continued

Important Marker: Scaling and revenue increase – business booms.

Once you've been established for a while and all your systems and strategies are running like a well-oiled machine, your business will begin to really thrive. Therefore, your business will experience a rapid growth in revenue and cash flow. This is what I call the Exponential Growth Stage – it's the time when you get to reap the benefit of your proven sales model, marketing model, and operations models. If you do the system right and adapt and tweak your business towards growth through all key stages, then you will experience Exponential Growth.

Now once the 10 strategies are optimised to their fullest potential this usually results in a $1-million dollar per chair practice.

If you have found yourself in the Preparation Stage, and have never made the leap to the Exponential Growth Stage it's usually because you've been distracted by systems, or paralysed by them and have never progressed into full optimisation of all 10 strategies.

The 10 Strategies are responsible for your accelerated and exponential growth, together with the great leadership, innovation and marketing skills you have now acquired.

Plateau Stage

Period: Should be brief, ready for new growth.
Important marker: When you have maximised your growth.

The Plateau Stage is when you have maximised your business growth. It's the result of a natural business cycle—and gives the business an opportunity to reflect, grow and evolve.

Plateaus are vital to a company's development, and a successful company will experience them. The plateau is a chance to ensure all the systems and strategies are in place and you're preparing for a new growth cycle. With the right approach, you can ensure it's a marker for continued growth.

For a dental practice when you hit a plateau due to maximising your growth potential, this usually sits around the $1 million per chair practice, however in saying that, keep in mind that if you have three dental chairs — that means $3 million and four chairs equals $4 million etc.

PART 3

THE 10 GREAT STRATEGIES TO EXPONENTIALLY GROW YOUR DENTAL PRACTICE BY DESIGN

10 STRATEGIES

1. Marketing
2. Top Telephone Techniques
3. Seven Star Customer Service
4. Case Conversion
5. Treatment Coordination
6. Follow Through
7. Referrals and Reviews
8. Recare
9. Branding
10. Dashboard

BECOME A DENTAL MARKETING MACHINE

STRATEGY #1: MARKETING

I'm going to say it straight up. This is the most important strategy to know!

Think of an archery champion wanting to hit the bullseye – where do they aim?

So if you want to hit your own bullseye in life – aim for it.

Marketing helps you hit your target.

International archery champion Larry Wise explained the mindset and mechanics behind hitting a bullseye to upcoming archers recently. He said, "If you don't have a plan, you plan to fail." He said, "You need to keep a journal of what you did with what arrows, and trace where you went amiss or did better."[27]

---

27. The Gazette, Jessica Cohen, published online Jan 4, 2019, www.recordonline.com/news/20190104/world-archery-champ-imparts-art-of-hitting-bullseye

He advised his students to set goals and write out a game plan to achieve them.

Coming from a world champion – they listened.

You market in the same way. You aim for what you want. You make a game plan to achieve it and you test and measure what did work and what didn't.

Let's begin with your website.

A BUSINESS WITHOUT A WEBSITE IS A BUSINESS THAT WON'T LAST LONG

Some dentists think 'Why should I invest money into a great website if I don't work online?'

Here's a few reasons:

- Your website reflects you as a business owner and professional.
- 80% – 90% of people use a search engine to find a local product or service.
- A good online presence can improve your credibility instantly. In fact, around 84% of consumers reported that businesses with a good website were more credible than those with poor or no websites.
- You will get more guests coming to your internet home than your real home.
- You will grow your business enormously if you have a highly-optimised attractive website.
- All your leads from AdWords, Google, social media, will come through your website.

But to be really blunt, in the words of Bill Gates, "If your business is not on the internet, then your business will be out of business."

Whether you like it or not, people will discover and make judgements about you from your website. After coaching and consulting with hundreds of dental practice owners, I have noticed that the websites which are very poor to average get poor to average results. If you do not get your website to be great, then you're missing out on hundreds of clients a year. Hundreds!

One of the most bizarre things I see in the dental industry is that most practice owners are okay to drive a fancy car or to buy a decent house. Some are happy to spend thousands of dollars on a great sofa in their home, or the latest designer furniture, whilst on the flipside they're getting the most intimate guests coming to the website and they're not willing to spend money. They're willing to spend peanuts on a place that hundreds of people visit. They visit it more than your actual bricks and mortar home.

Dentists must understand that most patients ringing your phone are coming from your website. And if you are getting 10 patients calling you per week, how many are *not* calling you? Some people forget to think about how many are not calling. You might be missing out on another 20 people not calling all because your website is mediocre but not great.

I'm not going to sugarcoat this – you must have a great website. You must make people feel 'at home' in your online home. You must furnish your online home just like you would your real home. It's a place for visitors.

The two most important things about a website are the:

1. Look and feel.
2. The influencing copy.

Most people are visual. Think about the colours of your website, the position of the buttons, the overall layout needs to be visually appealing and mobile friendly.

I have noticed that when most dentists outsource their website to be built, they just outline the description of the treatments and services they provide. The description tells you nothing about why they should be choosing *you* as a provider. You need to show your customers your WHY and their WHY.

Why should they choose you over another? Imagine there are 15 dentists all in a row. What makes you matter? What makes you stand out? What makes you the one to choose?

Your copywriting should reflect this. I help a lot of dentists in this area because it's notoriously missed. It's not deemed 'important enough' and yet it is vital. Writing a good influencing copy is a special type of writing. Think of it this way – everyone knows what a procedure is – information is easy get these days – you can google Wikipedia or read a "how-to" blog in minutes. Writing about fillings or veneers is not influence. Writing an interesting piece about what you do and how you do it is nice, but it's not influential.

Influencing copy creates emotion and stimulates action. A good influencing copy makes you want to press that link or make that call. It should invite action and prompt the readers in a specific direction.

I help Dentapreneurs build a great website with influencing copy because then they can double or triple the new patients they see without working harder. The website is the tool that is always selling your company whether you are or not. Without a phenomenal website, you won't grow a phenomenal business. Without suave influencing copy, you'll limit the amount of conversions from your website. You'll miss leads every time.

There are three main places you get traffic from your websites, these are: AdWords, SEO, social media (we will delve into that deeper very shortly).

If you think you can become a millionaire overnight, or if you think you can build a million-dollar per chair practice within months by spending pittance on advertising, then you're delusional.

I honestly mean no offense when I say this, but if you're not willing to invest in yourself and your practice with time, effort and money – I don't even want you to read this book. You won't get anything out of it. There are no silver bullets or gimmicks here, so you'll only be wasting your time.

If you're not 100% committed to throwing everything you have behind the success of your business, then I can't help you. It's all or nothing. I can only help you if you let me and also if you help yourself. It takes drive and dedication – you're either in or you're not.

Essentially, if you think about it – this book is all about marketing. You are a dentist already, now you need to learn how to market your skill, and fulfil your potential.

Your number one responsibility as the business owner is to grow your business and you cannot do this without marketing. Let's go through some website basics that can boost your business.

Now I understand that a lot of dentists balk a mile when I bring up marketing. Many don't understand it and find it confusing, or they have tried it before and it didn't work.

A colleague recently reminded me of the funniest 90 seconds of the movie *The Pink Panther Strikes Again* when Inspector Jacques Clouseau checks into a hotel in Munich Germany and attempts to get a room for the night.

> **Inspector Clouseau:** Do you have a rheum?
> **Munich Hotel Clerk:** I do not know what a "rheum" is.
> **Inspector Clouseau:** *[Checks his German translation book]* Zimmer.
> **Munich Hotel Clerk:** Ah, a *room*!
> **Inspector Clouseau**: That is what I have been saying, you idiot. A rheum. *[Gesturing to the hotel's dog]* Does your dog bite?
> **Munich Hotel Clerk**: No.
> *[Clouseau bends down to pet the small dog; it immediately growls and bites him.]*
> **Inspector Clouseau**: I thought you said your dog did not bite!
> **Munich Hotel Clerk:** That is not my dog.

That is how marketing is for a lot of dentists. They've been bitten before – they don't trust it. Much like many patients have been 'bitten' by other dentists too. They don't trust it won't happen again. The people you are selling to have been bitten and they have a belief that "all dentists bite."

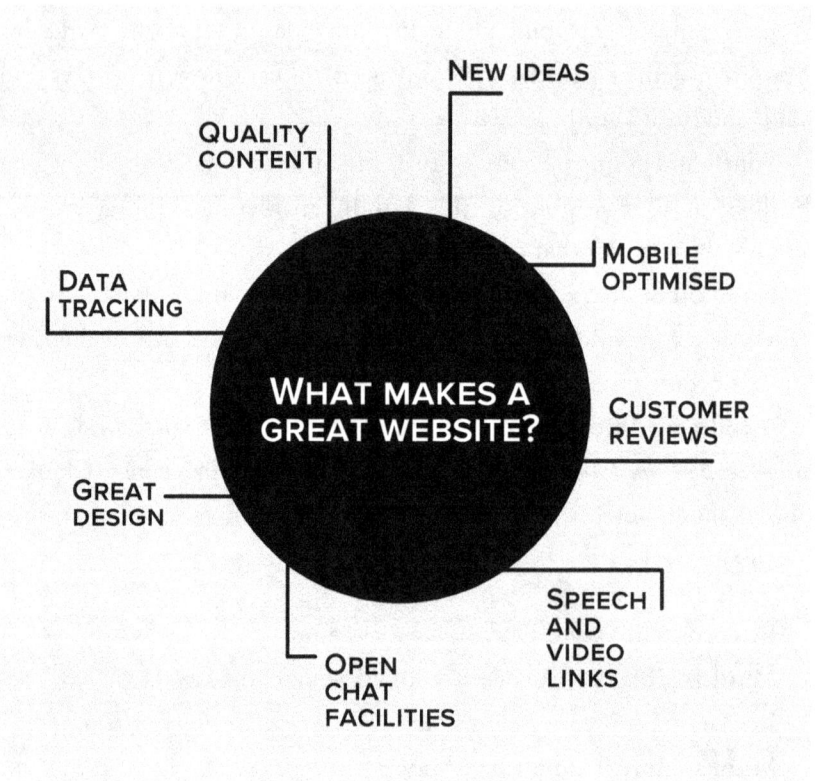

WHAT MAKES A GOOD WEBSITE?

A good website has:

1. A good domain name

Your domain name is part of your brand. It should be easy for a user to type it into a web browser or an e-mail address.

2. Great design and navigation

Use attractive and friendly images. May sure your website is up-to-date and easy to navigate. Have Call-to-Action buttons and ensure everything is easy to read and appealing. Ensure it is mobile-friendly.

3. Copy and content

Ensure you have fabulous copywriting that says who you are and why clients should choose you.

Use a professional copywriter that understands marketing. It's important to consider your client – use second-person pronouns such as "You" and "Your." Make sure your ad copy speaks to your customer rather than making it all about you!

- Break writing down into short paragraphs, with headers if necessary
- Use bullet points
- Highlight important words or phrases
- Be positive, welcoming and clear
- Use interesting blog posts or products links to optimise your SEO
- Join your social media content with your pages
- Utilise free content marketing like e-books and newsletters
- Use How-To guides and tutorials
- Include short videos and audio recordings
- Infographics or other visual content.

Basically why should they choose you compared to your competitor? What's unique about:

- Your practice
- Your technology
- Your clinical strategies
- Your team
- Your service
- Your products
- Your outcomes

These are the most important frames you need to have on each landing page. I help many dentists specifically on this so they can actively inspire many more new patients to call their practice.

4. Contact info

Display your contact information and a map of where you are clearly. Don't make your clients hunt for information. Make it easy for them to see you.

5. Your Team

People want to know who they are dealing with. Include a team page with all the people – the dentists, the front desk team, the dental hygienists.

6. Great images

It's important to use great imagery on your website. Show your practice, show your before-and-after photos. Don't try to do the photography yourself, hire someone who gets the best out of your business and make your website look and feel fantastic.

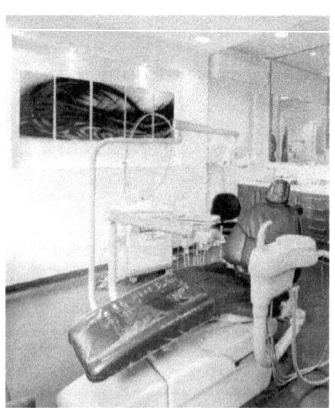

7. Testimonials

Include positive testimonials and reviews you have received from your clients. Everyone loves to know your customers are happy. Keep these updated regularly and use full names if possible. No one trusts that Mr X is happy with your service. But they do trust if Teresa Jones from Fremantle, Perth, is happy with you.

8. Call to Action

Tell your online visitors what you want them to do clearly. You may want them to call you now for free quote, or make an appointment online.

You can highlight your call-to-action by using special buttons or highlighting the text.

Now, that's a good website. But remember we want great, not just good.

A GREAT website has all the above but it SELLS for YOU!

A good website is lovely to look at. It does its job in terms of looking and sounding nice.

A great website however is active and actually creates leads and interest for you! There's a big difference between them.

A great website utilises extra tools so you know that your website is working for you.

Because whatever gets measured gets managed.

Always check your Google Analytics to see how many people visit your website versus how many actually schedule an appointment by completing a form. Or how many telephone calls come from your website.

A website is your second-home. It's where you need to look after your visitors and give them a wonderful place to visit.

Here are some of best marketing strategies I have used to grow my dental empire.

HOW TO GAIN HUNDREDS MORE LEADS IN THREE SIMPLE WAYS

Google AdWords

Google Adwords is an advertising platform based on "pay per click" (PPC) or "cost per click" (CPC). Unlike other PPC platforms like Facebook for example, AdWords offers advertisers two basic ways to reach people, through the Google Search Network and the Google Display Network.

Google Adwords use a bidding system, where advertisers bid to have their ads shown to their target market. Advertisers will choose the amount that they're willing to pay for a single action (like a click). They can also decide how much they're willing to budget for one campaign.

For example, you may bid to have your ad show up every time a user types in "Dentist in Northern suburbs Sydney." Or "Family Dentist in Hobart."

The Google Search Network allows you to show your dentistry ads to customers who are actively searching for the keywords that you've selected. So you really have to think carefully about what your customers would type in.

Make sure you don't use really broad keywords like "dentist" or "teeth whitening" or "filling". This is way too broad and competition is fierce.

Good keywords are more specific:
- Teeth whitening services in [location]
- Dental office in [location]
- Emergency dentist in [location]
- Dental veneers in [location]

REMEMBER: Do not target your entire city or state. Most people are looking for someone relatively close by. Be specific to your area. Think of your local suburbs.

Essentially PPC platforms can be done two ways: how much you bid on individual clicks or how much you can afford to spend on a single campaign (your total ad budget).

I recommend to many of my clients to not just think of profit per click or even the first sale of a new customer – but to consider the value of a client over the lifetime of their relationship with you. Compare this against your conversion rate and you'll be able to better assess how much you can afford to bid.

The powers of Google can match the wish of the searcher based on things like location, user history and past preferences. Google's primary job is trying to match the user's search with the right websites according to the user's requests, wishes and wants.

Keyword	Searcher	Cost
Family dentist	The searcher could be searching for family dentistry in a general sense (perhaps even for a friend or a school assignment). This search is considered a generalised type of search.	Low cost. This person/family may or may not be ready to book an appointment. It's less expensive if people are less likely to be serious or immediate buyers.
Family dentist Sydney	The searcher is clearly searching family dentists in Sydney. They're exploring the best options and seeing who looks friendly and where they are located. This type of search ranks higher because it is a more focused search.	High cost. Competition amongst family dentists in Sydney pushes the cost of this keyword up because the likelihood of the searcher/family being new clients are higher.
Book family dentist Sydney	This searcher is ready to book with a family dentist in Sydney. They're possibly ready to book for more than one person. This type of search ranks very high because it's exceptionally focused and immediate.	Highest cost. This person/family is ready to book an appointment. Competition for this type of search will be the highest and therefore cost more.

Adwords is useful for many reasons. They show up when your customers are looking for very specific needs or very specific locations.

Google Marketing Live 2019 event was an extravaganza of new possibilities for us in dental marketing. There are so many more advanced options to us now.

For example, the first ad in search results with Google Adwords have previously been text only, but now the #1 spot will be given images too. Local campaigns will have better reach with ads now appearing in the Google Maps search suggestions (based on user's search history, keywords, and other signals), and also while a user is using Google Maps for directions, travelling from one destination to another.

Going into all the possibilities of Google Adwords is truly an entire book in itself. I have used Adwords strategically for the last 15 years to achieve great results. If done right – it really works.

Here are a few quick tips on what to do right.

✓ Bid on Location Keywords

Bid on location keywords such as *dentist Greensborough* or *Redfern dentist* depending on your location.

The search quantities are likely to be less for keywords such as these, but the CPC (Cost per Click) is very likely to also be low. These are targeted searches for the high-quality leads without a massive expense on your behalf.

✓ Bid on Best Keywords for Your Business Type

Think about what your business is and who your target market is. Think about how you position your business in the market. Are you the family dentist or more a cosmetic dentist?

Think about what your customers would search for. It's much better to hit the bullseye once than try a million shots that never hit.

Your customers may want a dentist for different reasons.

- Appearance: they may type — dental implants, Invisalign, braces, whitening, veneers, cosmetic dentistry, fix my smile.
- Pain relief: they may type — dental emergency, 24-hour dentist, emergency dental work, toothache, tooth pain.
- Price-conscious: cheap dentist, cost of dental implants, affordable dentist.
- Locality: dentist near me, dentist reviews, family dentist.
- Family/children: dentist for children, gentle dentistry, braces for teenager, sedation dentistry, paediatric dentist.

✓ Utilise Your Demographic

You can target the right people for your business. Round pegs in round holes as they say. It's a better fit for them and a better fit for you.

For example, a dentist promoting family dentistry can target the ads toward parents, or a dentist working in cosmetic procedures can target the right age and income for that person.

✓ Include Google Ads Call Extension

Most dentists know that phone calls are very common in our industry, a lot of people book dentist appointments from a phone call. You can utilise a clickable call button using the Google Ads Call Extension so people can call your clinic directly. They will also be given an option to click on the ad or visit your website. This is a must in the dental industry.

✓ Use Google Maps

Showing your search ads on Google Maps is a great way to attract customers who are looking for a dentist near them. Remember people care about where you're located. Make it a no-brainer for them to visit.

✓ Think about Voice Searches

By 2020, 50% of all internet searches will be voice-based. Another way of looking at it is if you are not part of the voice search future, you are not part of the 50% of searches.

Currently there are only a small number of big players that we talk into, these are:
- Google Home
- Amazon Echo/Alexa
- Google Assistant
- Siri/iPhone
- Android Phones And Devices
- Microsoft Cortana

There are a few key differences between web search and voice search. The biggest difference being that voice search is conversational and consists of longer sentences. Web searches are very short and to-the-point, like the keywords we looked at before.

Voice queries for dental services will need longer keywords like:
"Where to get dental implants in Sydney"
"What does teeth whitening cost"
"Find my closest dentist"
"Need an emergency dentist in Melbourne CBD"

More than 15% of voice queries contain one of the following three trigger keywords these are: **How, What, Best.**

Here are the main current voice queries, though I suspect as voice queries grow, this list will also grow and change.

Trigger Words	% of Total
How	8.64
What	5.01
Best	2.63
The	0.98
Is	0.70
Where	0.57
Can	0.56
Top	0.55
Easy	0.41
When	0.36
Why	0.34
Who	0.33
New	0.33
Recipe	0.30
Good	0.30
Homes	0.28
Make	0.26
Does	0.26
Define	0.25
Free	0.24

Source: BrightLocal.com[28]

✓ **Adjust your Bids**

Advertising for dentists is better when you can show ads to people near you and let them decrease in frequency as the searches move further away from your clinic.

---

28. www.brightlocal.com/wp-content/uploads/2017/09/best-keywords-for-voice-search.jpg

Google Ads allows you to control the proximity and distance from where your dentistry ads are shown utilising Google's bid adjustments. You can bid higher for close proximity and reduce the amount you place on bids as the searchers distance themselves from your clinic.

GOOGLE DISPLAY ADS

Google Display Network is a network of more than 2 million websites and 90% of internet users that allow Google Ads to be displayed. This means that your dental ads can reach people while they're web surfing, watching YouTube or scrolling Facebook. The Search Network can reach people when they're already searching for a specific product or service or *before* they begin searching for what you offer.

Google Display ads are usually cheaper than Google Search Ads. Google search ads are entirely text but Google Display ads are images, so for dentists this can be a big advantage.

The great thing about Google Display is that you can select the domain names you want your ads to appear on (but that doesn't necessarily mean that you'll get them.)

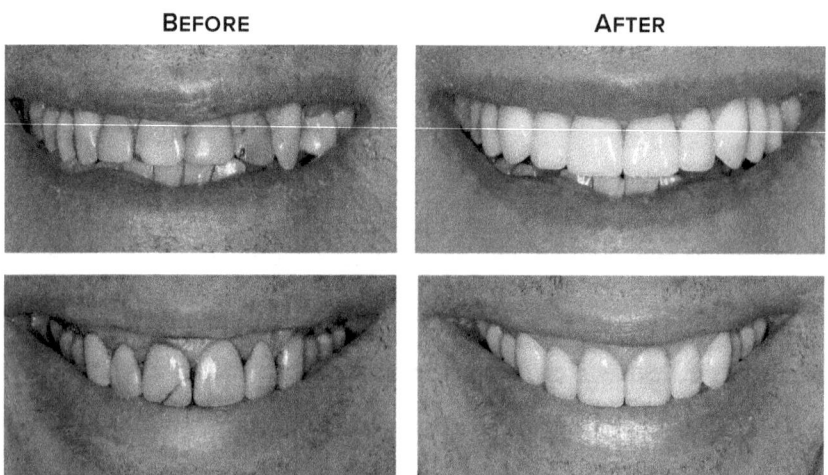

Source: Smile Concepts

Social Media

Social media marketing is the use of social media platforms to connect with your audience to build your brand, increase sales, and drive website traffic.

You can use social media to:

- Post before-and-after photos
- Include a short video tip
- Make an announcement
- Link to your blog article
- Post a funny meme to get smiles
- Show a behind-the-scenes sneak peek
- Answer FAQs
- Debunk industry myths
- Post an industry fact or statistic
- Solve a common dental problem
- Share a fun fact
- Reveal a new product on the market
- Reveal your new service or offer
- Post a positive testimonial or case study
- Promote your newsletter
- Run a contest
- Take a poll
- Mention an influencer in your industry
- Share some dental tips
- Post an inspirational quote
- Show smiles that happen after treatment
- Thank your followers
- Share a trending topic
- Share a printable download or content
- Highlight a National holiday or international event
- Ask your followers a question
- Reveal your advice on particular services

And so much more....

I always suggest to people not to post randomly and expect results but to be deliberate and create a social media strategy.

The first step to creating a winning strategy is to establish your objectives and goals. Without goals, you have no way to measure success your return on investment.

And the great thing about social media is you can measure a lot of it.

Here's a very simple social media strategy. Define:

1. Who is your target audience?
You can find out by answering these questions:
- Where is my audience?
- Where is my audience active?
- Where is my audience searching?
- What problems do they have?
- What do they want?

2. What are you going to share?
The next step is to determine where you are going to share your content, which social media platforms are best for your business?

Make a plan for your content. Chart your topic for blogs and your posts. There are great platforms now like Hootsuite where you can schedule your posting and it does it for you.

3. Where are you going to share it?
You don't have to be on every social media platform, just focus on the ones that work for your business. Before deciding, also consider exactly which time of the day and which days of the week you want to post, consider the behaviours of your target audience, what works for them?

4. Who is sharing it?
Who in your team is handling the social media? Or will you outsource to a social media strategist? Who understands what each platform can do?

5. When are you going to share?
What are the best times to post for your industry and your country?

6. How will you measure it?

Business Goal	Social Media Goal	What to Measure
Grow your brand	Increase awareness for your current and potential customers	Followers, shares, etc.
Turn customers into fans	Increase engagement (see how your customers are engaging with your content)	Comments, likes, mentions, shares, discussions, etc.
Drive leads and sales	Conversions (how engagement is converting to customers)	Website clicks, email signups, appointments, phone calls, etc.
Improve customer retention	Keep your customers happy and loyal and referring others	Testimonials, social media videos, before and after photos, referrals etc.

SOME EXTRA TIPS

The great things about social media is you can target patients close to your office.

Instead of distributing leaflets that people throw away or recycle, why not target your local community on Facebook and just inform them that you are in the community.

"Hey, I'm the dentist on Main St. If you ever need a dentist, you can quickly get help. Here's why you should choose us (and also a friendly discount because we're neighbours)."

It's cheap. It's easy to set up. It works.

Facebook/Instagram/LinkedIn/YouTube

You don't need to be on every social media site. But these big four are definitely worth considering.

Facebook – for ads and engaging with your community.
Instagram – for great before-and-after photos (especially for cosmetic dentists).
YouTube – for those happy to promote via video or give tutorials.
LinkedIn – for the professional network and business community leaders.

Facebook allows you to indulge in a whole swag of great strategies and posts. You can post and share industry knowledge and also provide some new learning avenues for your clients or potential clients. Remember to link back to your website in your post so people can go straight to your website. You can create your own advertising campaigns and become the go-to content creator for your industry – all at the same time.

As a huge proportion of people are visual learners, images to Facebook and Instagram accounts are great.

Facebook also has a feature called "Lookalike audience".

You can ask Facebook to find people that "Look like" my general target audience. A "LIST" for Facebook is just a group of people who performed a certain action.

Here are some examples:
- people who visited your website
- people who completed a form on your website (you have to set up this conversion beforehand)
- people who watched a video
- people who engaged (liked, commented, shared) with your page.

Facebook will show your content **ONLY** to those people with similar interests, behaviours, demographics, etc. to the people from the LIST (or custom audience) you provided.

Because a lot of people give Facebook a lot of information about themselves, such as businesses we interact with, our marital status, things we like, photos we engage with, activities or businesses we are searching. These signals help a business target specific customers.

SEO

SEO is an acronym that stands for **search engine optimisation**. This means optimising your website to get un-paid traffic from the search engine results page. It's often misunderstood and in the dental industry – grossly underestimated.

Search engines are your friend. Their entire job is to provide the best searches and services for their users. This means delivering results on the search engine pages that are high quality and relevant to what the searcher is looking for.

The search engines robots have their own job, they scan countless websites to deliver the best results for people typing in topics or keywords.

For instance, if you have written a blog about what to know about getting dental veneers, in order for this blog to get "hits" you will want to optimise this blog so it will show up as a top result for anyone who searches for the phrase "getting dental veneers."

The rankings of these search results are determined by Google's algorithm. Although Google keep their algorithms secret, years of experience in SEO have given us some knowledge about how it all goes down in Google's SEO chamber of secrets.

Basically, there's two types of categories:

On-page SEO

On-page SEO factors are all those things you can influence from within your actual website. Things like:

Speed – In 2016, research showed that 53% of mobile website visitors leave a website if it doesn't open within three seconds. We all know this frustration.

Less dead links – Reduce the amount of dead-end links. Links that go nowhere or links you have forgotten to link with other pages.

Safety – Implement a HTTPS. This is a MUST these days. A secure site is necessary. You can easily see a HTTPS in the browsers, and this will reassure you of a website's safety. If you see the words "not secure" — this is a red flag that the website isn't secure. Make sure your website doesn't have this because it will scare people off using or exploring your site.

XML – Simply put, an XML sitemap is a list of all pages of your website. It's like a quick map for search engines to ensure they can see everything on your site. The sitemap is usually in sections like posts/pages/blogs/tags etc. It also identifies the number of images and the latest date that your web pages were modified.

A technically structured website is fast for users and easy to use for search engine robots to scan. A well-done website helps the SEO robots understand what a site is about and doesn't send them into non-working links or duplicate pages or insecure web pages.

You have to have both the technical aspects of a website (security, speed, XML) and the non-technical area of a website (colours/logos/branding) all working together.

Off-page SEO

In addition to on-page SEO factors, there are off-page SEO factors. These factors include links going to your site from other websites (like guest bloggers or influencers) or any social media attention.

The more quality, relevant sites that link to your website, the higher your position in Google.

In SEO, strategic links from other significant websites sends a message to Google that says: "Great, other websites are linking to this website, it must be good. It can be trusted."

So, the Google Kings rank it higher.

Off-page SEO also include celebrity endorsements and influencer links.

For example, teeth-whitening entrepreneurs Nik Mirkovic and Alex Tomic who founded the company, HiSmile, in 2014 with just $20,000 of their own money to now around a staggering $100 million, built their brand from celebrity endorsements and the Influencer community.

Nik Mirkovic said they "decided to get very meticulous with our marketing approach by incorporating influencers in different regions to share their HiSmile experience, in doing this we were able to build brand transparency and trust with our customers fairly quickly."[29] And that 'fairly quickly' was in fact rapid in most people's eyes.

But that's what focus and calculated risk for return can achieve.

Many dentists don't even think beyond the average customer – you can use outsider influence too.

Yes, celebrities endorse their dentists and let's be honest getting a "Hollywood smile" is a very trendy thing to do.

STAY ACTIVE AND FRESH

There are many benefits of SEO for your business, for instance it can improve your visibility, engage potential clients and increase your chances of traffic. But remember the more quality, and relevant your content the more likely search engines will rank your pages higher.

Use relevant keywords that a searcher might type in when looking for dentists.

29. Retail Biz, Published online by Georgia Clark, September 2018, www.retailbiz.com.au/retail-profiles/hismile-capitalising-on-social-media-to-grow-a-100m-brand/

Another key factor for search engine ranking, is how fresh and current your content is. How often are you engaging and posting new content to your site?

You can also freshen up your content in a number of ways: rewriting old posts to make them more current, updating statistics, highlighting a current newsworthy topic and adding your latest photos.

A few helpful tips to rank higher:
- Write blogs around 2000 words, as they tend to rank better on the first search engine results page.
- Use images in your content, as posts featuring images receive 2.3 times better Facebook engagement.
- Don't be average – engage your clients with important relevant content.
- Before-and-after shots speak a thousand words. So use them.

HERE'S THE THING ALL DENTISTS NEED TO KNOW

Your highly-optimised website will increase phone calls. It's supposed to. Your Call to Action is contact. You want your customers to call your dental practice.

Your website is designed to make people feel comfortable, to engage them and ease their tension. And because it encourages friendliness – it will increase phone calls and this is a great sign.

Talking to people is the best and most valuable tool for a dental practice. We are in the people business. We are in the business of changing people's lives.

Marketing is not a gamble unless you don't know what you're doing and you're throwing money at a place when you don't know the rules of the game.

I can tell you that for every thousand dollars I spend on marketing, I'm getting 10 to 13 thousand dollars back in return. That's because I'm not gambling, I'm placing my money strategically and it is working for me. I want you to do the same.

Investing money is very different to gambling, right? One yields a return and the other is based around very uneven odds, usually against your favour.

Now, I know that some of you may feel overwhelmed and stampeded with all this tech-talk and SEO jargon, after all – you're dentists not digital marketers. It can seem a lot to take in initially. But here's the best part — you don't need to spend your precious time in SEO school and navigate an entirely new terrain. I'm not saying that you should put down your dental instruments and get out of mouths and into technology. I am saying that as the owner, you need to hire experts to do this for you. At the end of the day, you're a dentist and that's what you excel at – but that doesn't mean ignoring the business. It means getting smart and making sure your website, your SEO and your marketing is top-notch so you can be a happy, free and stable dentist not a time-poor, stressed one. There's a big difference between the two. Using this strategy will propel you into "happy dentist" terrain and that's where you will stay.

What if I told you that you'd get an extra 30-50 clients per month simply through utilising your marketing capabilities – would you take it seriously and do it? You'd be damn foolish not to, right? 10 new customers per week is a healthy and very accessible amount. I work with many dentists that begin to see these results once they get the gist of what to focus on.

Let's number crunch here. 30 new clients per month is 360 new clients per year. 50 new clients a month is 600 new clients per year.

Now, imagine you turned away 600 new customers from your business, people would say that you were crazy — but that's essentially what you're doing if you ignore your marketing capabilities.

Because this area became such a massive part of my success, over the years I've spent an incredible amount of time learning the ins-and-outs of it. So much so that I went and started another business called DigiDental (digidental.com.au). I hired leading experts to provide specific marketing services to dentists – so they can stay in their lane of genius without missing out on the abundance of new clients. This digital agency, DigiDental, has been specifically designed to help dentists achieve their online goals and build a thriving business.

HOW TO CONVERT 85% OF YOUR CLIENTS USING ONLY YOUR VOICE

STRATEGY #2:
TOP TELEPHONE TECHNIQUES

Alexander Graham Bell wanted people to start conversations by saying, "Ahoy-hoy!" before Thomas Edison popularised the use of 'hello', which we've kept up with today.

If you call Russia you may get *'Ya sluchu vas'* which translates to *'I'm listening to you.'* Or call Italy and you'll hear 'Pronto!' as the standard Italian phone greeting, and it means *'promptly'* – as in, speak promptly!

Point is – **it does matter how you answer the call** for maximum effectiveness. Ahoy won't cut it.

Like in the movie *Ghostbusters* the receptionist answers, "Ghostbusters, what do you want?".

And she could get away with answering that way because 1, no one else was in the Ghostbusting biz and 2, people calling needed to get rid of a ghost.

Dentists can't play by the same rules. Because 1, you have competitors and 2, you don't have ghosts haunting your clients.

In other words – just because someone calls your practice to make an appointment doesn't mean you'll have a new patient when you hang up. How you answer the phone and handle the call matters.

Social media and websites are great facilitators for helping your clients gather information and get a feel for your company, but meeting in person or talking on the phone really builds positive employee and client relationships. Don't leave this part to chance.

I'll say it again – you are in the people business. Not the teeth business.

The conversion rate from phone to the chair in most dental practices is around 40%. That's an annual statistic. I would say it's more likely around 30 to 40%.

Now, imagine someone wants to get some major cosmetic work done, they're going to call a few businesses. It's not a small decision for them. It's not just a filling. It's a big investment.

Now here's the thing, most dentists don't know the conversion rate from phone to chair. Why? Because they're not measuring it.

Why is the conversion rate so low? Because they're not providing adequate training.

As we say in the dental industry "where there's no pain, doesn't mean there's no pathology." If there's no pain, it doesn't mean there's no problem.

There's often a massive underlying problem. Just as we're saying to patients, if there's no pain doesn't mean there's no problem – it's the same for us dentists.

This is why I believe wholeheartedly in using telephone scripts. To be deliberate in what you say and how you say it. In my workshops, we role play them. We don't just answer the phone without intention or without intentional service.

To be honest, the real conversion rate should be around 80%. That's what we have measured. A good telephone script is not just a recital – it's a unique and meaningful way to engage with your clients. To help them feel safe and heard and comfortable with you as their chosen dentist.

Now, here's something every dentist needs to know:

Nowadays, approximately 40% to 50% of phone calls coming in now are cost related. Most people are price conscious. If you haven't trained your team to handle these questions – then you are missing out big time!

Remember, those customers are going to go and see a dentist. You must know how to handle all these pain points in your customers and address them effectively.

To increase your phone conversion from 40% to 80% – you must be trained and deliberate. I have tried this strategy for over ten years, I can honestly say – **if done correctly it converts 85% of the time.**

So – BE G.R.E.A.T.

GREETING

Get it right from the get-go. The first 30 seconds determines the future of the relationship. You can't afford to be complacent. This initial greeting is a highly sensitive moment and it needs to be treated with respect and thoughtfulness. The aim should be to impress them by showing warmth, care and understanding. It's not just a 'hello' – it's an intention to help and provide them with knowledge and a safe environment for their needs.

RAPPORT

Building a rapport means to create a common bond of trust. It is the foundation of a long-term business relationship. Showing genuine interest in each caller and listening to their needs whilst addressing their problems with professionalism and sensitivity builds trust and helps establish that firm foundation. They must know they are in good hands.

ENGAGE, EMPATHY, ENDORSE

Engaging your client on a call is very important – no one likes to speak to a boring disinterested personality. Engage your potential client and ask genuine relevant questions. Display authentic empathy, it's not easy for many people to go to the dentist, it's important to be sensitive to their needs and exude empathy toward them. Empathy is what makes us all human and it's a natural trait to use when another requires understanding.

Endorse. Endorsing your dentists and their work is highly necessary. Everyone wants to know that the person taking care of them is qualified, professional and excellent at their craft. Endorse your team, endorse the treatment and the dentist. It's extremely reassuring and helps the treatments go well for everyone.

ASK FOR AN APPOINTMENT

Now it's time to set an appointment. We use a specific strategy in doing this to ensure they attend and we don't have a diary full of cancellations. (we discuss this in depth in this chapter).

TAKE INFORMATION

Take the important and relevant information required. Take a deposit and clarify everything for the client in a personal but professional way.

IF YOU MISS THESE 3 THINGS – YOU MISS THE CUSTOMER

Your team needs to know in the first two minutes how to **engage**, **show empathy** and **endorse** your business. This is critical and it should happen before you relay information about the cost of your service.

My dental practice name is called Smile Concepts and once we were at a stage where we were getting 220 new patient phone calls per month. 220 new phone calls, and our conversion rate was approximately 175. An 80% conversion rate.

A lot of practices I coach are averaging about 60–80 new patients a month, but the great ones are over 100. Now that's possible for everyone.

Our primary practice is a four-chair practice grossing $4.3 million. Hence, that's an average of $1 million per chair. Often, other dentists ask me – what's your secret? I tell them I focus 80% of my time on only 10 strategies.

Now, the thing to know is, if people are taking the time to call, they want something. They aren't just picking up the phone and calling dentists because they're bored. You must be attentive to their needs. They need some questions answered, they need reassurance. They need to know you are there for them.

If you fail to train your team in **Engagement, Empathy and Endorsement** – your conversion rate will remain at 40% or lower.

Let's do a little role-play…

The caller is named Julia and she is enquiring about a dental implant. Now, imagine Julia calls an untrained dental practice called Dr Great Teeth. They are all good technicians but they're terrible at marketing. In fact, they haven't even thought about their dental bullseye.

Here is how it goes down.

Receptionist: Hello, Dr Great Teeth Dental Surgery, how may I help you?
Julia: Hello, I'm just enquiring about how much your implants generally are?
Receptionist: Sure. Our implants range from $__ to $__ depending on the amount of work you need.
Julia: Ok, great. Thanks. I'll have a think about it.
Receptionist: Sure. No problem. Have a great day.

Epic fail.

Now, if Julia were to hang up and then call our practice – Smile Concepts, this is how it would go down.

Sylvia: Welcome to Smile Concepts Dental Surgery, this is Sylvia speaking. How may I help you?
Julia: Hi. I'm calling to know how much you charge for an implant?
Sylvia: Certainly I can help you with that. May I know your name, please?
Julia: Julia.
Sylvia: Julia, may I ask why are you looking at getting an implant done?
Julia: Yeah. I just feel like my teeth are moving and I just want something in there.
Sylvia: Oh, yes, that's important. Julia, may I ask any other reasons you're looking into getting an implant done?
Julia: Because my teeth are moving I'm worried one will come out and affect my smile.
Sylvia: I can understand why that's important to you Julia. Of course, we can help you with that. Julia, just to let you know that Dr. Shah does our implants, he has been experienced for 18 years and doing implants for the last 18 years. And just on a side-note, we do something here called digital guided implants.

This is just a tiny taster of the difference a trained staff member can make. Instead of giving a random cost, we choose listening and empathy. Build rapport.

It's important that you get to know them as a person and understand their unique needs.

THE GO-SET-GO TECHNIQUE

TELEPHONE PRACTICE IN DENTAL PRACTICE

1. **Sit up** straight and **smile**.
2. Welcome to XYZ Dental. You are **speaking with ABC**. How can I HELP you?
3. **CERTAINLY** I can help you with that,
4. May I know **YOUR NAME?**
5. So Mr/Mrs/Ms...

Let's look at that call again with some extra notes in italics. Some additional hints.

Sylvia: Welcome to Smile Concepts Dental Surgery, this is Sylvia speaking. How may I help you?
[Engages with name and introduction, wanting to help]
Julia: Hi. I'm calling to know how much you charge for an implant?
Sylvia: Certainly, I can help you with that. May I know your name, please?
[Answers positively and asks for name]
Julia: Julia.
Sylvia: Julia, may I ask why are you looking at getting an implant done?
[Engages and asks]
Julia: Yeah. I just feel like my teeth are moving and I just want something in there.
Sylvia: Oh, yes, that's important. Julia, may I ask any other reason

you're looking into getting an implant done?

[Empathy and understanding]

Julia: Because my teeth are moving I'm worried one will come out and affect my smile.

Sylvia: I can understand why that's important to you Julia. Of course we can help you with that. Julia,

[Empathy, understanding]

Sylvia continued: just to let you know that Dr. Shah does our implants, he has been experienced for 18 years and doing implants for the last 18 years. And just from a side note that we do something digital guided implants here.

[Endorsement]

After Sylvia has **endorsed** our service and dentist, she **asks** for an appointment.

We don't leave appointments to chance either. We have a phone script for appointments too. As so many dentists do this wrong and get more unattended appointments than any other industry.

We also use scripts for discussing the payments procedures. At Smile Concepts, we even take a deposit (see Strategy #5 for more details).

So, I guess if you haven't heard me say it ten times already – Are you taking the bull by the horns and being deliberate in every step?

For face-to-face workshops, specifically on crafting the best telephone techniques for your company go to **kinnarshah.com/events**.

Or get in touch with us to help you train in-house at the comfort of your dental practice.

I've helped lots of teams increase their new patient conversion rates to booking by over 80%.

WHY TRADITIONAL FIVE-STAR SERVICE IS OLD-FASHIONED

STRATEGY #3:
SEVEN-STAR CUSTOMER SERVICE

Let me share a story about Martha and Stumpy. Martha and Stumpy went to a carnival and at this carnival there were joy flights – adrenaline-filled airplane rides where the pilot does drops and turns and circles.

Stumpy kept saying to Martha "I want to go onto this plane ride. I want to have a joy flight."

Martha looked at the plane twirling in the sky and said, "No. No. We can't go it's too dangerous," and Stumpy kept saying, "I want to go."

Martha said, "No, Stumpy. It's very expensive. We can't."

Stumpy said, "No Martha. You don't understand, I really want to have a go." Stumpy became very persistent about getting a go on this aeroplane.

Finally, a nearby pilot overheard Stumpy's persistence and their bickering. He walked up to them and said, "Listen. I'm going to take you up for free, but I don't want to hear a single word out of your mouth. I'll only take you for free if you shut up."

The pilot took them on the ride and he was silently thinking in his head, "I'm going to have some serious fun with these two." He took his plane up really really high and quickly dipped a steep left, then he flew down and down and took a sudden steep right.

They didn't even scream. No noise. The pilot thought "Hey, how come these guys are not screaming?" So he became more aggressive in his flying. He went up even higher than before and took a steep sudden left, then a sudden and swift right. No noise at all. Not a single word.

When he landed the plane back on the ground, he turned around and said, "Oh, you guys were amazing. Not even one sound. I've never done this for anyone else, but it was one of the most fruitful rides ever. And you guys didn't even make a noise."

Martha turns around and says, "Well, I was going to say something when Stumpy fell out."

The moral of the story is – **give all patients a fun and fruitful experience and don't lose them on the way.**

What gives your business the wow factor? The double-wow factor?

This is where seven-star customer service comes in. Most people claim to give four to five-star service, but in this arena of hardship, economy and competition, we need to step up and stand out. We need to be seven-star givers. Five star is the old way of doing business.

Yes, you must step up and stand out. You do this by being a seven-star business, not a five-star.

An Italian restaurant opened up next to my house a few years ago and we went with the whole family. The restaurant was only about a month old at the time.

We were met by a fancy Italian waiter with his authentic Italian accent. "Buongiorno. Buongiorno."

He greeted us and helped us to our table. He went through the daily specials, and what wines were good, he made a few jokes and we chatted easily.

I was already convinced that it was five-star service. But what he did next, is what I call seven-star.

He disappeared with our order and literally a couple of minutes later came out with four freshly-cooked small dumpling-looking things. He placed them on the table and said "The chef is trying out something new today and he would love your opinion on them."

That is seven-star service.

Now to be honest, I don't remember the meal I ordered, or whether the food was good or not, but I left with a great experience of service and care. And do you think I went back and told my friends about it? You bet I did. I've even told thousands of people this small story because it's what I remember.

You see the small things between five-star service and seven-star service make the difference. They stick in your mind and you don't forget.

Here's some tips of small things that are the big things:

TIP #1 – THE WARM GREETING

When a new patient walks into your practice, ***don't*** do what most do. It usually goes something like this...

Client: Hi. My name is James. I'm here for my 2:00 appointment.

Reception: Hi James. Just fill out this form and bring it back to the counter when you're done.

If you walk into Smile Concepts, Sylvia or one of our team would stand up and come around the desk. We would shake your hand and say, "Welcome, James. My name is Sylvia. Welcome to Smile Concepts, I will be looking after you today."

Huge difference.

Two of my favourite airlines are Singapore Airlines and Emirates, and if you have ever travelled business-class with them, you know it's a cut above the others. I often think of how we treat our patients should always be first-class, we shouldn't even have an economy class.

I want you to think about what are you doing at the moment. Is it first-class or economy service?

TIP #2 – USE LOVE LANGUAGE

Use love language. Language that is open and supportive and kind.

Thank you.
My pleasure.
Certainly.
Of course we can help you.
You're welcome.
Great question, I'll find that out for you!
I can understand that's important to you.
Excellent.

Never say:
I don't know.
That's not my problem.
That's not my job.
It's policy. There's nothing I can do.
Just look on the website .
I don't see your information in our database.
Can I put you on hold?
Hang on. My computer is running slow.
That's not my department.
Can you call back later?
Just a sec while I ask someone else.
What's your name again?
Calm down.

> *"The difference between the almost right word and the right word is really a large matter — 'tis the difference between the lightning-bug and the lightning."*
> *Mark Twain*

TIP #3 – GIVE THEM TEA, COFFEE

Many people relax with a nice warm drink. Offer them tea or coffee. Or there may be times when the dentist is running a bit late so offering them something while they wait is polite.

TIP #4 – INJECT A LITTLE HUMOUR

Now, I know you're a dentist not a stand-up comic, but who doesn't love to smile and laugh?

Being at the dentist isn't the way people want to spend their day, so what can you do to make it a little brighter and a little less intimidating?

You don't have to have your punchlines ready to go, but maybe you can inject a little humour into your waiting room or in your surgery centres.

I've seen a great dentist with an oversized *Where's Wally* on his roof. Or a Wi-Fi password that was 'flossdaily' with a little sign that added 'no caps, no spaces'. Or a dentist mug that said, "I create beautiful smiles, what's your superpower?"

Here are some dentists that have injected some humour into their practice.

Humour that won't work – (even if you have a laugh)

Remember, like all strategies – it's about getting it right because getting it wrong is detrimental to your company. Like these below. I'm not sure you'll win many extra clients this way.

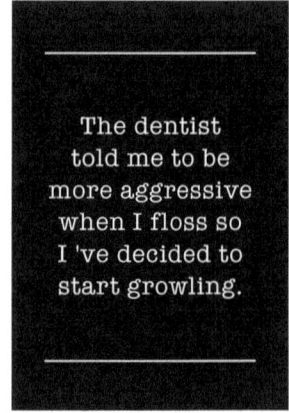
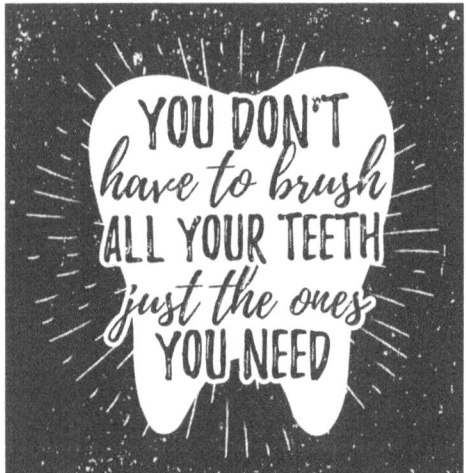

This is an example of what not to do.

Patient: It must be tough spending all day with your hands in someone's mouth.

Dentist: I just think of it as having my hands in their wallet.

Or

Dentist: This will hurt a little.
Patient: OK.
Dentist: I've been having an affair with your wife for a while now.

Or

How did the dentist become a brain surgeon?
The drill slipped out his hand

Anything that emphasises pain, drilling or horrible experiences is best left unsaid.

TIP #5 – OFFER A WET TOWEL

Ever been on a plane or in a restaurant and they offer you a nice fresh warm wet towel? It's refreshing and feels lovely. You know the classy type you get from airlines and high-class restaurants.

Imagine you've got a cleaning done or a filling done. You feel better when you can freshen yourself up, wipe your face and hands in a lovely warm towel.

TIP #6 – OFFER EVERY NEW PATIENT A GIFT

Give your new patient a little gift to say thank you for choosing us. We often give one of those high-grade aluminium water bottles, or maybe you can think of something your patients would love and appreciate.

A recent study by Dr Robert Cialdini revealed that shoppers at a candy store that received a free sample of chocolate upon entering were 42% more likely to purchase candy than those who did not receive a gift.

However, there is a caveat to this – the gift must be meaningful, unexpected, and customised.

In another of Cialdini's studies about tipping, diners at a restaurant in New Jersey who received a piece of chocolate with their bill increased their tips by 3.3%. But when diners were given 2 chocolates, the gift seemed to suddenly have more meaning than just one and the tips increased by 14.1%.

Now, this is not to suggest that you give a gift or two to get something back – you don't. You give a gift to show appreciation. But gifts seem to make everyone (including the recipient) feel generous and happy. Be a giver!

Tip #7 – The Exit

Walk your client to the door and open it for them. It's not hard to do. It's simple and yet getting rarer these days. We would say:

"Looking forward to seeing you (name) and looking after you next time."

Seven-star service is not difficult. It just needs to be in place. It's so simple that people forget to do it, or don't think it's that important.

And here's the bottomline – people want to have a great experience! Remember that. Ask yourself – how can I make this wonderful for my clients?

Did you know:
- 75% of people continue to spend more because of a history of great experiences.
- More than 80% are willing to pay more for the great experiences.
- More than 50% who've had great experiences are three times more likely to recommend your company to others.[30]

---

30. Customer Experience Insight, Published online by Michele McGovern, April 9, 2018, www.customerexperienceinsight.com/the-nicest-things-you-can-say-to-customers/

For face-to-face workshops on customer service and utilising the best techniques for your dental practice, go to:

kinnarshah.com/events

Or contact us for a specialised and customised event at your dental practice.

Kinnar is sharing more in his INTERACTIVE book.

See exclusive, behind-the-scenes videos, audios and photos.

DOWNLOAD free content and learn how to exponentially grow your dental practice.

deanpublishing.com/dentapreneur

"Set your mind on a definite goal and observe how quickly the world stands aside to let you pass."
Napoleon Hill

SKYROCKET YOUR BUSINESS WITH THIS MILLION-DOLLAR FORMULA

STRATEGY #4: CASE CONVERSION

Now, let's be frank. Most dentists feel comfortable telling someone they need a filling or a clean. If someone only needs a small job done, most dentists have no concern offering a treatment plan and recommending what needs to be done.

Many dentists I meet are proud of their conversion history for small dental work. Yet many I meet are not making enough revenue. That's because you're converting too many small cases and missing the rest.

If you've come to a dentist and you need a filling done, you won't question it too much. If you're buying a pack of chewing gum you won't question it too much, but if you are spending $5,000, it's a different story. You care much more.

So what is the average conversion rate of the medium to high-end cases? Again, most dentists convert 40% of big cases. The conversion rate for all the small jobs are around 80% for some dentists.

To exponentially grow or build your dream dental practice, or to reach a stage where you're doing a million dollars per chair, you have to have a balance of both small, medium and big cases.

Great Dentapreneurs want to serve more patients, they want to grow and give people the best of their skill. You can't give people your best if you're not doing any of the major work.

The major case obstacle I see between the small and big cases is communication.

Primarily, people do business with people they like and trust.

> *"All things being equal people will do business with, and refer business to, those people they know, like, and trust."*
> **The Go-Giver – Bob Burg and John David Mann**

The main driving factors for people around the small jobs are: convenience and cost.

The driving factors for the medium to high-end cases is: to know, like, and trust you.

They are poles apart.

And when people are spending a lot of money and it affects the way they look, they want to know – "Have you done this before?"

It's a critical element for them. They need to trust that you're good, that you can do the job and that you can deliver good results. You need to be serving them and providing them with seven-star service and seven-star trust.

> *"Trust is the glue of life. It's the most essential ingredient in effective communication. It's the foundational principle that holds all relationships."*
> **Stephen R. Covey**

You need to understand that sometimes the last place on earth a patient wants to be is at your practice. If they don't like or trust you – you're history.

And not just you – but your team. Reputation is everything. And the reputation of a company matters nowadays more than ever. Because of online reviews, people now are making judgements before they even see you. They are making decisions based on other people's opinions of you. Yes, even without people meeting you, they're collecting information about you and judging you on that.

You can be the best dentist with the lowest income solely based on handling a lifetime of small conversions.

As I have said many times, most dentists get caught, rightfully so, in investing in clinical skills and advancing their ability to perform procedures in the most productive way. I admire that, but if you can't use these skills to their full ability, you're not reaching your full potential.

Have you ever heard someone go on a date and say, "I'm so happy and excited about going to the dentist tomorrow."?

For many, it's one of the most fearful places people can go. It ain't a fun-fair. You need to switch on and think of how that patient would feel. For them to allow you to perform big and ongoing procedures – they need to know, like and trust you. Period.

Maya Angelou said, "I've learned that people will forget what you said, people will forget what you did, but people will never forget how you made them feel."

That's for sure!

THE MILLION-DOLLAR FORMULA REVEALED

I have invented a strategy called the GPS strategy. It's an acronym for the Great Profit Strategy.

It's like your GPS system in the car. When you are looking for direction or a location or direction, you type it in the GPS. The GPS shows you a fast route and a slow route. Let me ask you – who the hell takes the slow route?

This GPS is a pathway to a faster route or how to get your patients to say yes to your recommendations, and strategy is called the Great Profit Strategy.

Hundreds of dentists are already applying this with super successful results. Over the last three years, I've trained hundreds and hundreds of dentists in this exact strategy and it's changing the way they do business.

Now, these parts have to be followed in order. You cannot convert medium to high-end cases with any consistency if you skip through this section.

You must master this 4-step process if you want to transform your business. And by doing so you will increase your revenue, build a phenomenal business and have more freedom of time, money, and choice. That is all attainable through this GPS system. However, you must do the steps well to ensure high conversion.

ENGAGE

STATE

There are two attitudes you must adopt to get where you need to go. These are my go-to attitude boosters. They are:

1. Your state dictates your fate.
2. Your energy introduces you before you even speak.

Getting into a peak state and being filled with positive energy is crucial before walking in for a consultation.

STYLE

First impressions matter. Over 70% of your patients have a visual dominant sensory perception. How you show up, how you present yourself, what you wear – all matters when converting medium to high-end cases. Take an inventory on this. My specific advice during these current times is not to show up wearing tunics or gowns. Rather dress smart.

SMILE

We all know the power of a smile. I see too many dentists introduce themselves with low energy or even low enthusiasm. Great posture and a killer super smile is a prerequisite for building faster rapport.

GATHERING INFORMATION

SERVE

The best way I've found to follow your introduction is to get straight into asking your client, "How may I serve you today?"

Respect other people's time in this tech-driven and advanced world. Hold their attention and lead them through this GPS process of case conversion.

SPIN

Now let me remind you: the most powerful secret to inspiring, influencing and impacting other people to buy into your ideas, message or recommendations is by asking intelligent questions!

The biggest downfall I've seen amongst dentists when attempting to convert many medium to high-end cases is that they end up telling much more then asking.

The art of building deeper rapport and getting acceptance lies in the ability to ask this specific 4-part SPIN questions. I've been training dentists in these dental related SPIN questions for years with tremendous success. Gathering intelligence is a very crucial step of case conversion and if too often overlooked.

SENSORY ACUITY

This is the next level of communication expertise and having this knowledge will immediately elevate your case conversion skill.

The ability to figure out the primary dominant representational sense of your client from the 3 types – visual, auditory or kinesthetic means that you will have an advantage in building a strong deep bond with your patient as you match their style.

This is an art and yet easy to learn. I demonstrate this skill and coach dentists to use and eventually master this skill in my seminars.

DEMONSTRATE AND DISPLAY

SOLUTIONS

Options need to be provided very strategically. It's super important to have your client's X-rays and pictures (both extra and intra-oral) on the computer screen in front of them while consulting at this phase. As you know, a picture speaks a thousand words and this could be another game-changer for you with your consults.

Also having demonstration models as visual cues really helps. For patients to actually see the product and feel it, is ultra-important. Your clinical training allows you offer various solutions and planning, yet there is a very specific way to do this whereby the patient sees and feels your expertise.

SCREEN

This is where you do a thorough clinical examination. Most dentists are already great at this.

$

Yes, you are responsible for discussing the prices of various dental options. Even if it's an estimate. The mindset of people nowadays demands you talk about this and not brush it away for your clinical coordinator to go over. You need to have the ability to talk comfortably about the various costs of medium-high-end cases.

The biggest amount I had to ever discuss with a patient was close to $120,000 and if I didn't have the skill to do this properly, I wouldn't have been able to serve the patient.

Talking money demands confidence and respect and the ability to handle all objections is what I go over intensely in the seminars. Common objections such as:

- It's too expensive
- Can you give me a discount?
- I need to discuss it with my partner
- I have to check my schedule
- I need to think about it
- Aren't you too young?

All these objections have a specific strategic reply in order to overcome the objection and get their full commitment.

CONVERT AND CLOSE

Satisfied

"What questions have you got?" instead of "have you got any questions?" is a very different way of asking.

This is a simple but powerful verbal technique to use before you convert and close. It brings about the opportunity for the patient to ask anything they are not clear about so that you can address it immediately.

Summarise

There is a very special NLP technique to be used here. It is a way to summarise all that's been addressed by bringing up 3 specific statements of acknowledgement.

SELL, PACE AND LEAD

Most dentists I've seen never ask for any sort of commitment!! I wonder why?

Asking a patient for their commitment is nothing to be ashamed of. I believe if you have the ability to serve someone with your skills, then ask for their commitment to your recommendations or at least the next step of further investigations. Asking for commitment is a must!

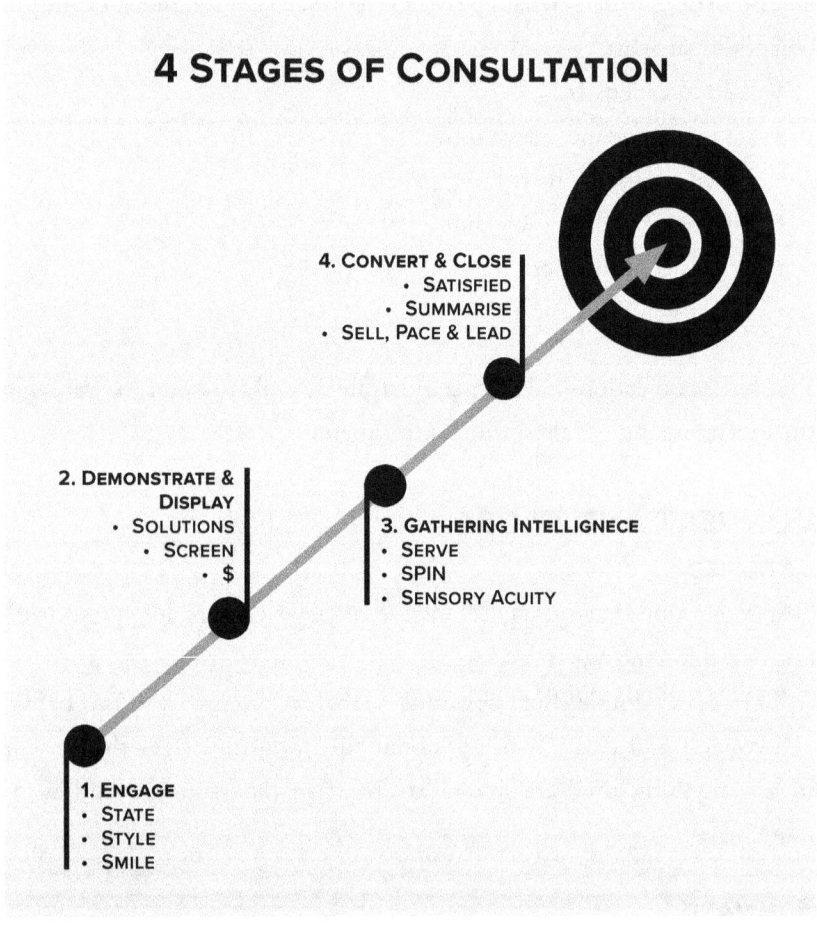

To learn each step and each strategy effectively, you can come to my workshop on this exact process and you'll boost your conversion rate exponentially.

NEVER HAVE MISSED APPOINTMENTS AGAIN – HERE'S HOW...

STRATEGY #5: TREATMENT COORDINATION

Treatment coordination is the crucial moment in which your patient exits the consultation with you and is now convinced that you are the right choice. This is when you hand him/her over to your team.

All team members need to internalise the different steps to a point where it comes absolutely natural to them to finalise the appointment and get a solid commitment in form of a deposit and a date of treatment.

Many people are commitment phobic – they avoid locking anything in solid.

Many people say, "Let me get back to you, I don't know my schedule."

A significant percentage of patients get lost at this point of the patient experience.

The common things heard by the front team even after they've said yes to you in your consult room and agreed to go ahead with you at the treatment coordination stage, they tell your front team that they want to think about it, or they want to check their schedule, or they want to discuss it with their partner.

And hence they leave without making any commitment, and most of the times they don't show up.

This particular strategy is to make it as strong as possible for the patient to make a commitment and not leave it to hope.

So, the million-dollar question is – How do you do that?

THE HANDOVER

You must handle the handover.

Let me give you an example.

"Hey, Sylvia. Bob has agreed to go up with the 10 veneers, so we're going to transform his smile. Yes, Bob, yes?"

Notice that it's "Yes, Bob."

I ask Bob to follow the 'yes' commitment by nodding and saying 'yes'.

I turn to my receptionist and say, "Sylvia, that's fantastic. Please arrange the necessary paperwork. Bob, I'll be looking forward to seeing you next time."

That handover is critical. Even just the simple things like saying that Bob has agreed to go with this.

I look at Sylvia, and then I look at Bob and say 'yes'.

How effective is that simple handover?

And then Sylvia would say, "Okay. My pleasure, Bob."

And I will walk away to help the next customer.

THE TAKEOVER

From the handover comes the takeover.

Sylvia would say, "Bob, how was your consultation with Dr. Shah?"

The first thing she'll do is ask you a question.

Ask question. "How was your appointment with Dr. Shah?" Sylvia would say, "Fantastic. All right Bob. Let's go over what Dr Shah recommended as a treatment. Let's go over your plan of the veneers."

By that time, it's been printed out, she goes over the plan and tells you what the final cost is.

"This is the cost. Dr. Shah said this would be done over two appointments, and so do you have the ability to be able to do two appointments?" Bob nods.

"The first appointment is a two hour booking and there's a deposit of $500 for that to secure your appointment."

The word we use is 'to secure your appointment'. We educate our clients to understand that the time is exclusively booked for them with Dr. Shah and their deposit goes towards their treatment.

I call it the **SET principle – Secure, Exclusive and Towards**.

Now, 90%–95% of practices don't take deposits. It a major pain point for most dentists. Many people don't show up if they haven't handed any money over.

You're booking that and when people don't show up at your appointment it hurts your business. When people pay a deposit, they are serious.

In our practice, 99.9% of patients have to leave a deposit or they don't get treatment.

If a client said, "I need to look into my funds," I'll say, "Fantastic. I'll temporary book you an appointment. This will remain active for 24 hours. What time tomorrow morning can I call you? I can take a payment over the phone."

And they usually say, "Okay. 10:00 in the morning."

We will call at 10 am.

The whole idea is that if you want to grow this practice, all these strategies need to be in place. You can't be sitting idle for one hour, because as dentists, if you're sitting idle and people don't show up, your business can't be sustained.

You need to have less cancellations and more serious appointments. Simple.

So we go over the treatment plan, book an appointment or break down multiple appointments and leave a deposit.

OFFER APPOINTMENT TIMES

"Bob, the first appointment is two hours long. We have next Thursday or the following Friday at 2:00 pm. Which is best?"

You see, a good dentist is highly-sought after and they won't be sitting around idle waiting all week for one person.

After the appointment is made, deposit is paid, we sign the consent forms.

Then once we've got it, we will say, "Bob, I put everything in a folder for you. Is there anything else you would like me to clarify for you today, Bob?"

By this time, hopefully Bob says, "No. Everything's been smooth. You have been amazing."

"Fantastic. Thank you, Bob. I put everything, all the information for you in a folder here. All your copies of the consent form. Your appointments are booked. And as a token of welcoming you to our practice, here is a little gift for you."

We give a classy aluminium water bottle as an appreciation gift. And then we stand up and I walk them towards the door to exit.

A great treatment coordination stage is very effective. It uses the right words, uses the right tone, and offers seven-star service.

IF YOU DON'T FOLLOW THROUGH, HOW CAN YOU EXPECT THEM TO?

STRATEGY #6: FOLLOW UP AND FOLLOW THROUGH

Now, let me ask you this. If you like someone, like you really like them romantically—you may have even gone out on one or two amazing dates, do you just leave them alone? Or do you call and speak to them? Do you make sure they know you're interested in them?

Now, I'm not saying a dentist should be romantic – I'm saying you need to follow-up and check in on your clients. Care about them. Show them you are interested. Ask them how they are, check if they're happy.

"Hi Mrs Jones, it's Kinnar from Smile Concepts, I enjoyed seeing your smile transform with your new veneers. I just wanted to check in and see how you are enjoying them? How are you feeling?"

Follow up allows you to monitor your clients' health, which is what you do, right?

It helps you reinforce any important knowledge and/or action plans. It helps engage and schedule any future appointments. It helps show them that you care. It helps with referrals. It helps with building your business.

You can't expect return clients if you don't follow through. Period.

I'd like to say that the three most important things about following up is to:

1. Follow-up
2. Follow-up
3. Follow-up again.

Do not make this an after-thought, don't just give it a try now and then when you feel like it — make it a strategy that you always do.

If you don't follow through with clients – how can you expect them to follow through with YOU?

I often tell my fellow Dentapreneurs that the **fortune is in the follow-up**.

People in business often avoid following up because they don't want to be a nuisance or be seen as pushy. And no one wants to appear like a desperate and dodgy salesperson. We've all been trapped by pushy salespeople – and no one I know likes it. But following up actually does the opposite of that: it makes you appear more professional and considerate. And inevitably, this will get you more clients and help you have a following stream of them. You don't need to be pushy, you just need to care. Following up with your clients is the art of true care.

According to mega research team, Salesforce, 92% of all customer interactions happen over the phone. That's one massive statistic every dentist must sit up and listen to.

But here's the startling opportunity. Salesforce also showed that 85% of potential customers are not satisfied with their experience over the phone. (salesforce.com)

In other words, most people don't know how to talk to their customers in a way that makes them feel heard and understood.

That gives you a great opportunity. If 85% aren't happy with their experience over the phone – the chances of you being the opposite and converting those unhappy callers into happy customers is very high. All you have to do is nail the craft of the call and the follow-up.

Now, before you start ringing all your clients or start calling up all those missed appointments or enquiries from the past 12 months – just know that around 63% of people who have requested information about your company may not make a buying decision for at least three months, and a further 20% often take more than 12 months to make a buying decision.

In other words, you can't win them all. BUT are you even trying to win? Are you actually following up and following through on a built-in business strategy?

And if you're not – you must! As I have said before, the fortune is in the follow-up. In doing what so many businesses fail to do.

Following up is essential to walking your talk. You say that you're excellent at personal and individualised patient care – but following up shows that you are.

Because the bottom-line is: if you don't look after your patients then someone else is going to. And if they do it well – you may never see them again. You can't afford to blow it because in this competitive era there are often no second chances.

THE TOP 5 THINGS YOU MUST FOLLOW UP AND FOLLOW THROUGH ON

The follow up isn't just a nice moment after treatment. That's one style of follow-up but following up is really a gathering of information on things that didn't work, not just things that did.

There are no good excuses for NOT following up. You may think there are some but I can guarantee that you're just believing your own excuses. You see, some people don't want to look at the reasons things in their practice aren't working, they don't want to uncover the flaws in their business and find out the reason why clients aren't returning or even turning up. If this is you – I beg you to stop it now. This type of behaviour will see you lose clients, money and a great future in business.

Throughout my time in business, I have honed down the top 5 areas that are critical to follow-up. Now, you and I both know that every area is important – but these are the ones you simply cannot turn a blind-eye to.

1. Telephone calls that were not converted to customers
2. Treatment plans not converted to customers
3. Reviews promised but not completed
4. Follow ups after clinical treatments
5. Follow up on important milestones of patients

If you ignore these top five areas, you ignore immense opportunity to learn about your clients' needs and therefore how to grow a booming business.

Let me ask you this, how many opportunities for new clients are there already in your practice? How many people have you not followed up? These aren't people that have 'rejected' you or one of your team, they are people that can tell you why they didn't choose you, or why they didn't attend their appointment or why they didn't complete their treatment plan. This type of feedback is gold! It gives you the chance to rectify the situation, to offer them a return visit, to find out the reason behind their behaviour. It gives you the chance to understand clients' objections and seek to resolve them sooner.

You see, following up and following through isn't something people often do, so if you do it often, you're going to get delightful unexpected results.

I'm so surprised how hard people work for one new client and yet they may have twenty potential clients that they haven't followed up.

I'm also surprised by how often I have to remind dentists that adequate follow-up is your responsibility as a health care professional. You are taking care of people's oral health and that doesn't stop when they walk out of the door.

According to the Australian Bureau of Statistics in 2017-18, nearly 30% of people who needed to see a dental professional either delayed seeing or did not see one. And furthermore, people were more likely to delay seeing a dental professional in the last 12 months due to cost than any other health professional.

Almost 23% of people aged between 25 to 44 years, delayed seeing a dentist, or did not see one due to cost, the highest of any age group.

So, you need to stay in touch with the obstacles people are facing and come up with solutions. Perhaps you offer payments plans or make a long-term health care plan. The most critical part is to stay in touch with them and find out their needs and their objections.

Don't be afraid to build a relationship. If they are celebrating a birthday or they have just had a new baby, keep in touch and see them as a lifelong patient – not just a one-time visitor. These are people you are honoured to look after, so take them into your life and value them.

It can be a difficult task to convince people how important oral hygiene and good dental health is. You can't just pull out a statistic and say, "Hey, did you know that across Australia there were 67,060 preventable hospitalisations for oral health conditions in 2015-16".

People won't care about your stats, even if it is true (which it is). People are concerned when they are one of the numbers, not when they aren't.

You can't go around convincing every one of the importance of oral health, but you can at least understand that many can't afford what they need. It's up to you to bridge the gap and help them understand.

To find creative ways around and through the myriad of reasons why people don't follow through on their treatment plans. And this is one of the reasons I always stress the importance of learning effective communication skills, because without them some dentists find the follow-up and the follow through difficult.

But I can guarantee that if you master the art of communication regarding the follow up and the follow through – you will immediately alter the nature of your business. You'll discover things you never knew and you'll have more success than you thought possible.

TIPS FOR THE FOLLOW UP AND FOLLOW THROUGH

HAVE A CLEAR GOAL BEFORE CALLING OR REACHING OUT

Set your intention first. Are you ringing to:

- See why they didn't go ahead with the treatment plan
- Ask why they didn't leave a review as they had promised
- See how they are after their treatment
- Follow up on a query they had.

Your goal should be focused on the needs and interests of the person you're calling. Now of course, there are certain telephone strategies for mastering the art of the follow-up – you don't just come right out and say, "So, Helen. Why didn't you show up when you said you would?" That would be a little too aggressive and demanding. You're not going to win over clients with that attitude.

You may instead say, "Helen, we noticed you didn't make your 3 pm appointment today and we were quite concerned. Is everything okay?"

Your client will be able to tell whether your follow-up was genuine or just a general company spiel. Put consideration into your question and be warm and open-hearted in your approach.

Engage and Empathise

Understand and listen to their needs. What are they sharing with you? Can you help them overcome any objections?

Offer solutions of how you can help them and genuinely listen to their replies. Listening is the key to understanding. Perhaps you can.

Ask About the Next Action Steps

Discuss the next steps. Are you booking in an appointment? What action is being taken? Are you calling them back again?

Have a plan for what comes next. Each patient may be different depending on their needs but you need an intention to get some momentum. Following up and following through is all about creating momentum and getting things moving in the right direction.

Say Thank You

Don't overlook the simplistic power of a *thank you*. Thank them for their feedback. Let them know that by being open and honest with you, they help.

Use Multiple Channels

Social media, email, phone calls, and even handwritten notes are all great ways to follow up with your clients.

Your client may be too busy to pick up the phone, but often have time to check their email or scroll through their Facebook account. Connect with them in a way that's convenient for them. Find out their preferred method of contact.

Now, this doesn't mean you want to overwhelm people with a Facebook message and a call and an email all at once. It's just to be mindful of their preferred method of contact and use it in a way that makes them feel comfortable.

Track your results to know which ways are best for each client. That way, next time you follow-up or they call about an appointment, you know exactly what they prefer. You can even say, "Mrs Johnson,

I have in my notes that your prefer to be notified by SMS for your appointment, is that still your preferred method or would you like me to give you a reminder call?"

Use Your Unique Selling Points

Every business owner has their own unique selling points. Your follow-up communications are the time when you really need to know these.

This is where you can really get into the details of your follow-up and explain why you can help them and the benefits they'll experience.

Follow Up the Follow Up

Reminding your potential clients (and existing ones) of what you can do for them whilst making it as personal as possible can really help increase your conversion rate and maintain happy clients. Keep a record of conversions and take time to really understand each client as a person and an individual. As I've hammered on about throughout this book – you are in business of people.

You need to know why people do and don't use your business. There are so many people out there waiting for you, invite them in to build or continue your working relationship together.

Don't just follow up once and think your job is done. Follow up and follow through as a continual practise. It's really a journey of business discovery if you do.

THE NEW SUPERPOWER TO YOUR SUCCESS

STRATEGY #7: REFERRALS AND REVIEWS

"People influence people. Nothing influences people more than a recommendation from a trusted friend. A trusted referral is the holy grail of advertising."
Mark Zuckerberg, CEO of Facebook

Yes, a trusted referral is the Holy Grail. You didn't even market yourself, someone did it all for you. That's priceless. Word of mouth is still one of the leading sources of business for small businesses. When a customer is ready to see a dentist, they often start by asking family members or friends who they go to. Alternately, they may have heard someone talking about their amazing dentists who gave them a new smile.

A recent study showed that when a dish was labelled "most popular" it increased sales of that dish by 13 to 20%. And that's just a dish of food. Imagine a dentist with great communication skills, a warm and kind and popular dentist – how many people would prefer to see that type of dentist?

Nowadays many people go online and look for ratings, reviews and comments posted on social media pages or google reviews.

As a small business owner, you probably realise that those personal reviews, testimonials and any raving reviews are gold for your business. They help you acquire customers without marketing. But what if you're not getting referrals?

The first thing you must do is **be worthy of referrals and reviews.**

This should be a no-brainer, but the problem with our world today is that people love to also leave bad reviews – because the keyboard warrior is more powerful than ever before. In fact, people are 52% more likely to post a negative review than a positive one.[31] So every single positive experience or review is priceless. One bad review on a site with poor traffic can be enough to prevent people from visiting your dental practice.

Consider these stats:
- 95% of respondents who have had a bad experience said they told someone about it, compared to 87% who shared a good experience.
- Friends or family were the most commonly told, (81% of those with bad experiences told friends and family) and (72% with good experiences told friends and family) then followed by co-workers (57% shared bad experiences and 40% shared good experiences).[32]

---

31. Dimensional Research® – Executive Summary, Customer Service and Business Results, Sponsored By ZenDesk. April 2013, www.dimensionalresearch.com
32. ibid

To be worthy of great review and referrals you need to:
- Be transparent – don't have hidden costs or extra charges you didn't discuss
- Go the extra mile and make your client happy
- Give a small gift to new clients
- Ask them if they are happy with everything
- Follow up and follow through in all areas.

BE DELIBERATE IN THE REVIEW CYCLE

Referrals and reviews don't happen by default. At Smile Concepts we like to ask: How was your experience with us?

It's an important question, a very important question. But we don't just stop with the verbal feedback, we like to document it. We share with our clients that we are proactive in building our online presence and ask them to please write about 6-7 lines of feedback. We ask them to please do it then and there on the spot. We send them a link and ask kindly if they would please do this before they leave. Naturally, we thank them and gesture our appreciation with warm smiles and handshakes.

I often tell my fellow Dentapreneurs to encourage their clients to write a review on-the-spot whilst the mood and energy is high. This is the best time and it saves chasing them at a later stage if they forget or get busy. We send a little URL link to the clients' phones so they can instantly open the link and write a review before they leave.

TURN VERBAL TESTIMONIALS INTO PUBLISHED ONES

If a customer praises your work but has to leave quickly and doesn't have time to leave a review – ask them if they would be happy to share that wonderful feedback. If they say 'yes' then type out the comment and send it to them via email, along with the link to post it. Make it super easy for them so they can just copy and paste.

You can also ask them for permission to post the comment as a testimonial on your website. It's important to know that 44% of costumers don't trust reviews that weren't written within the past 6 months[33] – you need a lot of frequent, recent reviews.

Reward customers who refer new customers to you
Maybe set up a reward scheme or a gift for every referral. Perhaps you offer them a special treatment discount or give them something special.

Deal quickly and proactively with any complaints
You don't want to leave problems fester. Deal with them proactively and quickly. Provide solutions and eliminate any negative feedback.

Strike while the iron is hot
Once the dental work is finished, be sure to ask their feedback to ensure that they are happy. If you wait too long, their happy mood may have subsided and your chances of following them up are radically reduced.

Make it as easy
For the client, writing a review isn't always simple. Some people feel awkward writing things, or awkward using technology. They may ask – where should I post it? What should I say? Do I need to create an account? These questions can feel like obstacles to some people.

Make the follow through easy for them. Give them clear and direct instructions on what to do and how to do it. Give them some examples of what other people have said and tell them the time it will take, e.g., less than two minutes.

> *"One customer, well taken care of, could be more valuable than $10,000 worth of advertising."*
> *Jim Rohn*

---

33. BrightLocal, *Local Consumer Review Survey, written by Rosie Murphy*. Published online December 11, 2019. www.brightlocal.com/research/local-consumer-review-survey

If you still think reviews aren't a massive part of our business, check out these incredible statistics from BrightLocal.com.

- 86% of consumers read reviews for local businesses (including 95% of people aged 18-34)
- Consumers read an average of 10 online reviews before feeling able to trust a local business
- 57% of consumers will only use a business if it has 4 or more stars
- 80% of 18-34 year olds have written online reviews – compared to just 41% of consumers over 55
- 91% of 18-34 year – old consumers trust online reviews as much as personal recommendations
- 89% of consumers read businesses' responses to reviews.[34]

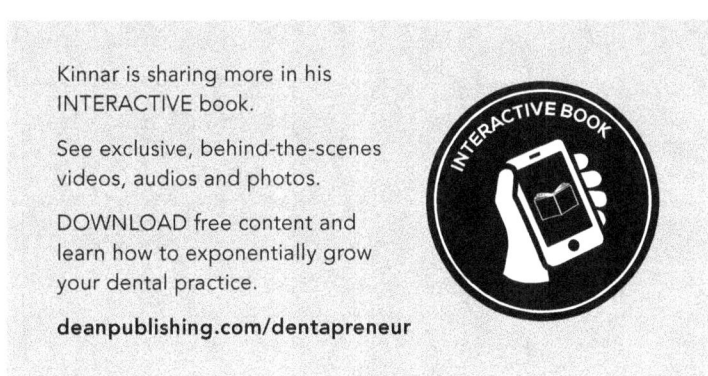

34. BrightLocal, *Local Consumer Review Survey, written by Rosie Murphy*. Published online December 11, 2019. www.brightlocal.com/research/local-consumer-review-survey

> "The higher you want to climb, the more you need leadership. The greater the impact you want to make, the greater your influence needs to be."
> *John C. Maxwell*

HOW MUCH YOU CARE ABOUT THEM IS HOW MUCH THEY CARE ABOUT YOU

STRATEGY #8: RECARE

Dental recare is the strategy or process a dental practice uses to schedule follow-up appointments for continued care.

So why is recare so critical to your success?

#1. It's a good way to make sure your schedule is full and productive thanks to returning patients.

#2. Patients tend to delay diagnosed treatment. An appointment with the hygienist gives them valuable time with the doctor to discuss why the treatment is necessary and shouldn't be delayed any further.

#3. You keep being on the patients' radar thanks to regular check-ups which retains them from going somewhere else.

To integrate a good recare strategy into your daily routine, you have to make it a habit and be consistent until it becomes an effortless task. Yes, RECARE is a habit for your business.

How to effectively use the RECARE strategy.

1. Software

I have yet to find software that does not have a way to capture and retain your recall patients. It is important that it is set up properly and that all users are trained on the correct use of the software.

Too often I see handwritten lists of patient names, with notes about calls made to those patients. This is because the user wasn't trained, doesn't trust, or finds the computer difficult to use. This is a waste of time and effort when there is technology that can take care of all of this in a nanosecond.

The other problem I see is people using the strategy incorrectly because they were taught wrong, or perhaps they were self-taught.

I cannot emphasise enough the value of training.

2. New patients

As soon as someone enters the practice as a new patient for possibly an emergency, the doctor should discuss the importance of a follow-up hygiene appointment. This is a step that is often overlooked. Again, the software can help make this a simple process.

3: Pre-appointing

Pre-appointing in hygiene makes life much easier on the entire team. It should be noted that consistent reminders help patients remember their appointments that were scheduled six-months ago.

4. Follow up

Follow-up (which means working the reports and making the calls) is the most mismanaged step in all recall strategies. The most popular excuse I hear is, "No one has time."

Statistics show that it costs **three times as much to find a new patient than to retain patients.**

5. Contact

It's important to be flexible and allow for multiple ways to communicate. Research has indicated that using different channels of communication can boost the effectiveness of dental recall a staggering 85%.

Use their preferred methods of communication – not the one your business uses. Think of them first.

6. The Right Communication

It is crucial to focus on how to put your point across with every patient. The right communcation makes all the difference. Using "love language" and caring words can put your patient at ease. It's important to discuss their health and oral hygiene in a way that is helpful, not harmful; even when you're treating a problem or preventing the progression of a problem.

7. Phone Conversation for Front Team

This is an example of a perfect phone conversation to book a recare appointment with a client:

> *"Hello, Mrs Smith. This is Sylvia from Smile Concepts. I'm so glad I was able to reach you today. Our records show that your last professional clean and check-up was back in February. As you may already be aware, your current dental cover allows for two check-ups and cleans every year. As it's now September, we thought you may wish to take advantage of your cover, as they don't carry it over to the next year. Most of our patients choose this option so they don't miss out. Our hygienist Megan has time next Monday at 1 pm and Wednesday at 10:30 am, which of these appointments suit you best?"*

8. Treatment Coordination

After the whole treatment is finished, the patient needs to be integrated into the existing recare strategy. This is a big challenge since for the patient the treatment is now finished and many patients don't find the value in following up every 6 months.

A great way to do that is to explain the benefits of pre-appointing. Let them know that your hygienist schedule fills up quickly and if they postpone you might struggle to book them in at a later point.

If they book the appointment today, they can always reschedule later down the line. An example for this conversation could be:

"Hi Mrs. Smith, I would like to schedule your next dental appointment on a day and time that suits you best. Would you prefer Monday at 2 pm or Wednesday at 10:30 am?
(Suggest the same day and time of their current appointment.)
Great Mrs. Smith! You are scheduled for Wednesday at 10:30 am. We have reserved that time for you and we will confirm this appointment with you two weeks before your appointment."

1. Monitor Your Recalls

Measuring your hygiene recall rate is really important for your dental business. Don't put your head in the sand, remember – what gets managed gets measured. A measurement helps you see what's working and what isn't.

2. Marketing Through Recalls

Add something in the message that adds extra value and makes it even more worthwhile for the patient to see you again. Look after both your loyal and new clients. Make it attractive for them to see you again.

DENTAL RECALL: WHAT TO DO AND NOT TO DO

✓ Schedule their next appointment before they leave	✗ Don't be afraid to discuss their next appointment or call them
✓ Give them a reminder text or call before their next appointment	✗ Don't bombard them with over-the-top reminders every second day
✓ Give every new client a welcome gift	✗ Don't give up if you don't hear from them or they cancel
✓ Be friendly & empathetic	✗ Don't call & not leave a message
✓ Start with what's necessary & helpful to them	✗ Don't overcomplicate the procedures or overwhelm them
✓ Discuss their next appointment with a positive attitude and expectation	✗ Don't be overzealous by offering too many options or procedures
✓ Do keep in touch with them regularly	✗ Don't expect them to keep in touch with you
✓ Do look after your loyal and new clients	✗ Don't take your clients for granted

"Knowledge isn't power until it is applied."
Dale Carnegie

WHAT IS THE BRAND MOST DENTISTS RECOMMEND?

STRATEGY #9: BRANDING

There was a famous commercial in the '80s about a dentist. It showed the back view only of a very good-looking muscular dentist with tanned olive skin brushing his teeth with a towel around his waist. It said – "This man is a dentist so we can't show you his face on television."

It goes on to ask which brand of toothbrush a dentist uses? This add become ultra-famous and everyone knew Oral B was the "brand of choice" by dentists (even if it wasn't – the ad said it was and people believed it.)

This add did wonders for Oral-B and it didn't even show the man's face.

Many dentists think that branding is their company name and logo. But I want to clear that up immediately. Branding isn't your brand colours and fancy fonts.

A brand can be simply summed up as:
Brand = Branding + Interaction/Experience

Your brand isn't your logo or business name. In fact, it isn't any one thing. **Your brand is every-thing.**

Your brand is the perception others have of your company, service and products It's basically how people think and feel about who you are and what you do.

Branding is massive because you are a brand whether you mean to be or not.

Your marketing influences that perception, but your brand exists whether you actively market your business or not. If you're in business, you have a brand. Now, whether you allow your brand to operate by default or you do marketing to influence the way people perceive your brand – well that's in your hands.

Most major businesses use marketing to try and manage the perception of their brand – to influence the way people think and feel about their organisation.

Branding is the process of creating, maintaining, strengthening or changing a brand.

Branding is a powerful strategy used to influence and manage the way people perceive and respond to your brand. Acquiring loyal customers is what many successful businesses strive for, and that's what branding is all about.

One of the best images I have ever seen that explains marketing in a visual representation is by brand expert Marty Neumeier from his bestselling book *Zag* (see: martyneumeier.com).

As he says, "It simplifies (to the point of absurdity) the relationships among the disciplines of marketing, telemarketing, public relations, advertising, graphic design, and branding. What makes it more than a joke is the kernel of truth in each simplification."

1. MARKETING

2. TELEMARKETING

3. PUBLIC RELATIONS

A great brand is when everyone knows you're a great ~~lover~~. Dentist!

If you look at Apple, they are the megastars of BRAND done right. They elicit feelings from people about products. They engage and tantalise.

Now, I know you may be thinking – what does a dental practice and a superpower like Apple have in common right?

Well, if you study the best, you learn from the best. Apple have untangled a lot of the jargon out of their marketing. They don't speak computer talk even if they sell them. They speak to their customers directly in a language they understand. Apple customers aren't bombarded with words like megabytes or gigahertz, they get words that are relevant to the user. Here's an example taken straight from their front-page website:

'Apple software is powerful and intuitive. Our products are secure, reliable, compatible with any office environment and easy to deploy. And everything we make works together seamlessly, giving you a mobile experience that delivers the information you need when you need it most.'

Now, for pretty complicated technology – they make it so accessible and easy.

The experience of being at an Apple store is designed to feel great, to make you want to use the products and ask the "geniuses" who work there about the products. It actually makes you feel like buying.

In his book, *Descartes' Error*, Antonio Damasio, professor of neuroscience at the University of Southern California shows that the consumer's emotional response to an ad has a far greater influence on their reported intent to buy a product than does the ad's content. In other words, how you make people FEEL is critical.

Brain scan tests also prove that when consumers evaluate businesses, they primarily use the parts of their brain associated with emotions, personal feelings, and memories/experiences, not the section associated with analysis and facts.

People are emotional beings, not necessarily rational beings. How people *feel* about you and your company determines your success and your brand.

Think of Apple in this example, they aren't the cheapest, in fact, they are often more expensive than their competitors – but they have created a unique experience. They don't compete on price, they don't even discount. In fact, Apple relies heavily on two different strategies: product placement (mainly with celebrities and in popular shows) and the hype created by positive media reviews.

To show my point, here's what Phil Schiller, Apple's SVP of global marketing said in a federal court in San Jose. "Apple's employees work closely with Hollywood on so-called product placement so its gadgets are used in movies and television shows."[35]

"We would love to see our products used by stars," Schiller told the jury.

Now, of course, this is Apple. They can afford celebrity endorsements and media popularity, right? But what you may not realise is a lot of Apple endorsements are for free.

Schiller said that Apple decided not to pay for any advertising during a period after the iPhone was introduced in January 2007. He said, "We didn't need to." He read several great reviews from primary sources about the iPhone and iPad and confirmed that such positive media stories did a better job than advertising to build buzz.

In an interview with *Businessweek*, American film producer Gavin Polone said: "Apple won't pay to have their products features, but they are more than willing to hand out endless amount of computers, iPads and iPhones."

In fact, if you look closely, you will see many movies and sitcoms displaying the famous Apple logo.

---

35. Financial Post, published online August 11 2012, https://business.financialpost.com/business-insider/12-fascinating-examples-of-how-apple-product-placements-rule-hollywood

You see phenomenal brands take-off through people. People build the brand. People's perceptions and feelings build the brand.

Many people give great reviews because they want to. In this case, because they love Apple's minimalistic products. Because you can get them out the box and they work easily and seamlessly.

Despite Samsung actually selling more phones during the last months of 2017, Apple still managed to receive 87% of total smartphone profits. Why? The power of their brand. They have legions of hardcore fans. Apple endorsers unite.

You see, Apple know who they're talking to. They have positioned themselves perfectly in the market and now people and media sell for them. Sure, they market and look after their brand but the brand has become synonymous with an experience of being an "Apple customer."

When you know your people and your position in the market – business gets easier. It's no longer a game of hit-and-miss, it's strategic and targeted.

What customers see is – the brand or the tagline, the marketing campaigns and the ads.

But what they don't see is how the company has positioned themselves in the market place.

Jobs defined the position of Apple around simplicity, creativity and humanity. Then he communicated that positioning through marketing campaigns, like 'Think different' and the famous commercials "PC versus Mac".

To be a brand is all connecting the hearts and mind of people.

Margaret Thatcher once said, "Power is like being a lady. If you have to tell people you are, you aren't."

A brand is the same.

IF YOU DON'T THINK YOUR POSITIONING STATEMENT MATTERS – READ THIS

Pulitzer Prize winning journalist and *Washington Post* writer, Gene Weingarten conducted an experiment.[36] He enlisted the help of renowned violinist Joshua Bell. Now to give you a bit of background information, Joshua Bell is one of the world's best violinist, he is the winner of the Avery Fisher Prize for outstanding achievement in classical music and sells out concerts all over the world.

Weingarten organised for Joshua Bell to play incognito in an arcade area within the metro train station during the morning rush hour. Bell played six beautiful musical pieces on a 3.5 million-dollar violin for about 45 minutes. Being rush hour, many people were in line to walk past Bell that morning. 1,097 to be exact.

Some people slowed down, most walked past. Some threw coins. One man leaned against the wall to listen to him for three minutes before needing to leave for work. One lady recognised Bell in the last two minutes of his performance.

In the 45 minutes that Bell played, a total of 7 people stopped and stayed for a while. About 20 people gave him money as they continued to walk their normal pace.

That morning, the famous international musician collected $32. Not to mention without applause or recognition. Little did they know that only three days before playing in the metro station, Joshua Bell sold out at a Boston theatre at around $100 per seat.

So, what is the difference between the three days? One night he sold out his concert for more than $100 per head, days later he plays to over a thousand for free and gets a meagre $32.

Positioning!

You can be the world's best, but if you position yourself as a busker people will pay you like a busker and think of you as a busker – even if you're music royalty.

---

36. Weingarten, Gene, "Pearls Before Breakfast" *The Washington Post*, April 8, 2007 Page W10.

Position yourself properly. Change your mindset. Position yourself where you belong. The question is where do you position yourself? At the bottom, or at the top?

Are you going to remain settling for second-best? Or are you going to lift your game and stand up and stand out? The choice is yours.

Amazon's positioning statement is this:

"Our vision is to be the earth's most customer-centric company; to build a place where people can come to find and discover anything they might want to buy online."

What's yours?

POSITIONING STATEMENT SAMPLE

FOR _____ , _____ IS THE _____
     (YOUR TARGET MARKET) (YOUR BRAND/COMPANY)   (CATEGORY)

THAT IS THE _____
                     (YOUR POINT OF DIFFERENCE)

SO THEY CAN _____
                    (BENEFIT)

BECAUSE _____ .
            (CUSTOMERS' REASON TO BELIEVE)

> *"It is in your moments of decision that your destiny is shaped."*
> **Tony Robbins**

THE EAGLE VISION YOU NEED TO CONTINUALLY SUCCEED

STRATEGY #10:
YOUR DENTAL DASHBOARD

Have you seen the way airline pilots view the myriad of buttons and screens in front of them? They are always assessing the altitude, the flight path, the power of the engine. Now, it's not that they're in charge of everything. The engineers are in charge of the plane maintenance, the air-traffic controllers are in charge of the flight path, the hostess's take care of the passengers. The pilot flies the plane and keeps checking the dashboard – assessing and ensuring that everything is running smoothly.

Assessing your dental dashboard is the same. You don't do everything, but you are responsible for ensuring it runs correctly. And if you're business is heading in the wrong direction – you steer it back in the right direction. You have the controls.

This is what your dashboard is. Just a powerful easy way to see the bird's eye view of your business each month.

It's amazing that it takes only 10-15 minutes of your time per month to know:
- how many new patients you had this month
- how many new telephone conversions
- how many reviews you received
- how many ads worked from your allocated budget
- what your ROI was this month
- what your turnover was.

Some good things in life only take a short amount of time. Enjoying a great coffee. Listening to a great song. Kissing your partner passionately.

What if I told you it would only take 10-15 minutes of your precious time to see your business growth?

Would you do it?

If you really want to keep your finger on the pulse of your business – you must.

ARE YOU AN EAGLE OR AN OSTRICH?

Your dental dashboard is your eagle's eye view of your business. Throughout history, the eagle has been universally seen as a visionary, a symbol of strength and leadership. An eagle-eye view is the best way to get the full vision of how your business is travelling.

The 'ostrich-view' – however is the head-in-the-sand approach, this may delay looking at the reality momentarily, but in the long-run, it will not work.

It's very important to understand that having your dashboard sorted is the best way for you to see your results. Include your team and educate them on why it's so important to the sustainability of the business. Don't wait 6 to 12 months to look at your balance sheet, to know your profit and loss statements – you need to pay attention to your business growth every month. You need to see what is happening every step so you can adjust and make changes in the right direction.

You are the chief of your business – you need to take responsibility and look at it clearly. Focus on it and build it. This isn't a hard process.

A mere 10-15 minutes of looking at your monthly reports reveals the secrets of your business. It clearly shows you what is working and what's not working.

"Beginning today, set an intention and a relentless focus on living your life as the greatest person you can be, in all situations. Demand that you demonstrate a strength of character in such a way that you find pride in who you are, and that others see you as a role model."
Brendon Burchard

DON'T MAKE THIS THE END

Now, typically this is supposed to be the end of the book, but I don't want it to be an ending for you, I really want it to be a beginning. A new and exciting beginning.

After all, I didn't write this book to fill your brain with more information – that's not what you need. You have information in droves, you don't need another well-meaning person to fill your precious grey-matter with more book-style advice. Great information without action just sits in your brain as useless knowledge. Great information can only be seen when it's expressed in action.

Just like an inventor may have a brilliant idea to change the world but unless he or she actually gets up and gives it a shot – it remains in the brain of the inventor as only an idea, it stays in the 'One Day' mentality we spoke about earlier. It only truly becomes something useful when it's acted upon.

> *"Having the world's best idea will do you no good unless you act on it. People who want milk shouldn't sit on a stool in the middle of the field in hopes that a cow will back up to them."*
> ***Curtis Grant***

This book is actually not for reading purposes, though paradoxically, you do have to read it to see that it's really for inspiring deliberate action. Action that actually has a bullseye – a direction – a path for pursuit. Laser-focused action.

Small shifts can have powerful consequences. But nothing moves until you do. Nothing starts until you set it alight with action and keep adding fuel to its momentum.

Think about this: in 5 years' time, you'll be on this Earth for 43,800 hours. Now, what are you intending on doing with these hours? How are you spending them? Or will they just drift by like the other years and you watch them like passing clouds?

You see, five years is HUGE if you use it. You can literally transform your business in that time. Remember the chapter on 4 Stages of a Dental Practice? Did you notice those initial stages were only 1-2 years long? Why? Because if you know what to do, you just breeze right through the stages and head straight for growth and success. If you solely focus on the right 10 strategies you could be somewhere completely mind-blowing within 5 years. To be quite frank, you can end up somewhere completely different by using these 10 strategies for five months but I don't want to say outlandish things like that because then you may ask me what could happen if you used these strategies for five minutes.

And here's the crazy kicker: you CAN even change your business using one of these strategies for only five minutes. Sounds nuts, right? But how long is that call from a new customer? Is it five minutes? Probably.

So, even if you sit back and do nothing — at least commit to perfecting five minutes of your talk-time and go for better conversion rates. And the result from that 5 minutes of being awesome will be so thrilling that you'll think *'Wow, imagine the results that those dentists who committed to five months or five years are experiencing.'*

And for the diligent ones, the ones ready to live BIG and get big results; let me ask you this: Where will you be in 5 years? Where will your business be in 5 years?

Think about it seriously for a minute or two.

That's 1825 days filled with 'something'. And you can make that 'something' anything you like. The question is: what will you make of it? How will you fill those days?

As Zig Ziglar said, *'You don't have to be great to start, but you have to start to be great.'*

Are you ready to be great? Now remember great doesn't mean perfect. Let me spoil the party right now and let you know that you'll never get it perfect, it's not about creating the perfect business – that doesn't exist – it's about creating *your* PERFECT business. Designing *your dream* by determining *your* destiny and not leaving it to fate. That's what this is about.

Now those five years can dangle in front of your eyes like a moving carrot dangling in front of a hungry horse – you can always chase the carrot and never get to eat it. But that's not what I mean. I don't want you to create a five-year vision that you never live. I am asking to be deliberate and make sure you do.

And the only way to live that vision is to ACT. **And the perfect moment to act is NOW!**

I invite you to one of my exclusive seminars. If you have read this book, I want you to walk right up to me and personally introduce yourself. Actually – bring the book too! We will mark down the day you began to get serious about skyrocketing your business and becoming a Dentapreneur. We will actually write in your book and date the moment you changed your own life.

These 10 strategies aren't for me anymore, sure, they gave me great success and showed me the possibilities in life but I want you to experience the freedom and joy too.

Even though these 10 strategies continue to be in my dental business – I am not there to check on them every day. In fact, the beauty is – they run like a well-oiled machine whether I am there or whether I'm on a flight to the Bahamas. The entire idea is that they work when I don't. They work so I don't have to.

But I chose to work. I chose to work because I love what I do. It's my WHY. It gives me a thrill and gets me up every day to grow more and give more.

So, here's my challenge to you. If you decide to mark a date in your destiny. Come along to one of my talks or seminars and bring your book. Let's date the moment you begin your journey to greatness and stay in touch.

I guarantee that if you follow my program and keep in touch with the tools and systems I recommend – you will NEVER be the same person who walked in.

As I said at the start of this book – I know that it may sound to some that I make some big heavy claims – and yes, I do. I stand by these methods and I've watched them change dental businesses every day. Do you want to experience the ultimate 'before' and 'after'? Because just like the "smile before-and-after shots" we take of our happy patients – I take them of my colleagues and clients. But it's not to show off their new fancy dental work – it's to show off their business transformation! But their smiles are so bright from success that everyone notices the smiles too.

So if you're ready to ditch overwhelm of over-work to build a thriving dental practice – then jump on board. We're riding express to success!

George Bernard Shaw said, "Life isn't about finding yourself. Life is about creating yourself."

Begin today. Create your masterpiece and never settle for second-best. If building a business beyond your wildest imagination is something that you feel you must do because it's your calling in life, then let me assure you – **your dream is NOT for Sale.**

That's right, some dreams aren't measured by the value of a pricetag. In fact, worthy dreams are measured by an unrelenting passion that makes you pursue them despite logic.

Your dream isn't for sale, it's only to be pursued and lived. So, are you ready?

Join me and other Dentapreneurs so you can **Design Your Destiny and Not Live It By Default.**

Go to: **kinnarshah.com/events**

Contact us if you would like us to help you:

✓ Exponentially grow your dental practice by design

✓ Learn more about our seminars

Contact us if you would like to book
Dr Kinnar Shah for a speaking engagement.

kinnarshah.com
digidental.com.au
destinydesign.com.au
facebook.com/kinnar.shah.10

"My intention is to make you wildly successful."
Dr. Kinnar Shah

THANK YOU

I want to thank you for having the courage and determination to change your life. Because it is a choice that you made. You made the choice to ACT. To find a new way of doing things. And I want to commend you for doing what so many fail to do. Well done.

I don't want you to leave here with information you do nothing with. To make it transform your life and your business practise – you must ACT.

It's my honour, obsession and obligation in life to help others grow. It's why I get out of bed and do what I do. It's what drives me.

MY PROMISE TO YOU

For those Dentapreneurs who are serious about taking their business and leadership to the next level, I am offering an exclusive membership package where I go into these steps even further. Where I give you everything I possibly can, everything I know about building and sustaining a business empire. Everything that I couldn't fit into a 200-plus page book.

It's not only a pipe dream to have a dental empire, it's truly possible. I personally guarantee, that anyone who joins my Diamond Dentapreneurs Membership will elevate their business success to a new level.

In fact, I'm so confident that I am offering a **110% money back guarantee** if you don't get massive value.

But for those who are ready to grow exponentially – here's a taste of what you'll receive with a **DIAMOND DENTAPRENEURS' MEMBERSHIP.**

- ✓ Live seminars and workshops with international speakers – valued at $25,800
- ✓ Product discounts worth over $15,000
- ✓ Clinical training workshops worth over $10,000
- ✓ Mastermind meetups with industry elites worth $3750
- ✓ Monthly training resources worth $5000
- ✓ A clear blueprint to grow your business into a multi-million-dollar operation!

And because I know it works, if you're not fully satisfied and if you feel that you don't get massive value or a shift in perspective, strategy and action steps on how to elevate your performance to the next level – I will happily refund the cost after attending your first leadership module.

TESTIMONIALS

To read testimonials based on Dr Kinnar Shah's work, please visit:
kinnarshah.com/business-coaching/testimonials

ABOUT DR. KINNAR SHAH

Dr. Kinnar Shah is a triple-certified coach in performance, leadership and business.

Using his highly successful dental practice (Smile Concepts) bringing in 250 clients per month, he is a master in the theory, strategy and execution of dental practice growth.

Dr. Kinnar Shah has mastered the practical science of using persuasive techniques to achieve enormous business growth.

He has trained 1000's of students to implement simple strategies that help them overcome very complex business problems.

His clinic, Smile Concepts has seen a 700% growth in the last 3 years. He has documented the drivers of this growth and will share it with attendees.

- High-Performance Coach
- NLP Leadership Coach
- NLP Business & Communication

Coach
- Gallup Strengths Coach
- Founder of CreativeCoachingConcepts
- Founder of Destiny Design
- Founder of Smile Concepts
- Founder of Dentrapenuers FB Group

He is obsessed in creating opportunities for his clients in a very concrete way to immediately increase the quality of their life experience.

His purpose in this niche is to interact with his clients for the primary aim to stimulate, motivate and facilitate their advancement, performance and hike them to new levels.

Dr. Kinnar loves travelling and exploring different cultures of the world. In his spare time, he loves to read on motivation and self-development and laugh away on comedy channels.

He is a member of:
- Australasian Association of Orofacial Orthopaedics (AAOO)
- International Association of Orthodontics (IAO)
- Australian Osseointegration Society (AOS)
- Australian Society of Implant Dentistry (ASID)
- American Academy of Craniofacial Pain (AACP)
- American Academy of Cosmetic Dentistry (AACD)
- Australian Society of Computerised Dentistry (AuSCD)
- International Congress of Oral Implantologists (ICOI)
- Ozdent Email Study Group.

kinnarshah.com
smileconcepts.com.au
digidental.com.au

ACKNOWLEDGEMENTS

No man is an island. This has been true in my life. Without the love, support and encouragement of my family, friends and team, this book, and the success that I have achieved, would not be possible.

To my parents – my father, Dr Subhash Shah and mother, Minaxi Shah. I must have won the "parent lotto". You gave me the education, the opportunities, and the solid foundation from which I built my life. Thank you for your devotion, care and continual support. I am so thankful.

To my brothers – Dr Manish Shah and Vikit Shah — together we have built our dream Dental Practice by design and not by default. You are not only my brothers, you are my friends and business partners. What a journey to trek as ONE.

My family – my beautiful wife, Bhavini Shah; my daughter, Mahi; and son, Aveer. Thank you for your unconditional support and unwavering strength. You mean the world to me and I am forever rateful for such an incredible family.

Our team – to all our team members at SmileConcepts, CreativeCoachingConcepts, DestinyDesign and DigiDental. You are superstars and I'm truly v for your time, effort and love in building what we are today.

Dentapreneurs – to my fellow colleagues and Dentapreneurs. You are the reason this book exists. Thank you for listening, leaning in and learning. Your success is what makes me smile.

SAMers – to the Success Accelerator Mastermind group. What can I say? The name SAMers is special — it's an attitude, an experience and a way of life. Thank you for all your inspiration and friendship.

Publishing team – for their proximity and their love and faith in me.

Susan Dean from Dean Publishing for her support and belief in me. My Chief Editor, Natalie Deane, for helping me create this author legacy. The entire team for making this book possible.

Readers – thank you to all whom read this book, may you use these strategies and live the life of your dreams.

Special notes – thank you to bestselling author, Marty Neumeier for his generous permission in using his clever branding pictures, and to other businesses and research groups for their permission also.

END NOTES

1. Al-Mohrej, Omar A et al. "Prevalence of musculoskeletal pain of the neck, upper extremities and lower back among dental practitioners working in Riyadh, Saudi Arabia: a cross-sectional study." BMJ open vol. 6,6 e011100. 20 Jun. 2016, doi:10.1136 /bmjopen-2016-011100

2. Australian Bureau of Statistics: www.abs.gov.au

3. Australian Centre for Business Growth, 2018, "New study reveals why Australian SMEs fail " University of South Australia Business School, 20 November 2018, www.unisa.edu.au/Media-Centre/Releases/2018/new-study-reveals-why-australian-smes-fail. Australian Centre for Business Growth, image recreated with permission.

4. *Stache Magazine*, Oct 15 2019, 'How Many Small Business Fail in Australia'. Small Business Magazine, https://stachemagazine.com/how-many-small-business-fail-in-australia

5. BOQ Specialist, *Dental Practice Research Report 2016/17*, www.boqspecialist.com.au/expertise/dental-research-report

6. Bohn, Roger & Short, James. (2012). Measuring Consumer Information. *International Journal of Communication*. 6. 980-1000.

7. Interview by Natalie Clarkson, "Richard Branson: My four tips for growing a business", 3 June 2015, Virgin.com, www.virgin.com/entrepreneur/richard-branson-my-four-tips-growing-business

8. Developmental Readiness for Leadership: The Differential Effects of Leadership Courses on Creating "Ready, Willing, and Able" Leader, *Journal of Leadership Education*, https://aces.illinois.edu

9. GALLUP.com, www.gallup.com/press/176429/strengthsfinder.aspx

10. www.edisonmuckers.org/thomas-edisons-philosophy

11. Bill Carmody, Published online August 22, 2016, www.billcarmody.com/tony-robbins-explains-2-millimeter-shift-can-make-break-business

12. Development Dimensions International, *The High-Resolution Leadership Report*, www.ddiworld.com/hirezleadership

13. Konrath, Sara H., Edward H. O'Brien, and Courtney Hsing. "Changes in Dispositional Empathy in American College Students Over Time: A Meta-Analysis." *Personality and Social Psychology Review 15*, no. 2 (May 2011): 180–98. doi:10.1177/1088868310377395.

14. *Wall Street Journal*, "Companies Try a New Strategy: Empathy Training", Published online June 21, 2016, www.wsj.com/articles/companies-try-a-new-strategy-empathy-1466501403

15. Gallup 2017, *State of the Global Workplace report*, www.gallup.com www.gallup.com/workplace/238079/state-global-workplace-2017.aspx

16. Performance Accelerated: A New Benchmark for Initiating Employee Engagement, Retention and Results, www.octanner.com

17. Boag S. (2017) Conscious, Preconscious, and Unconscious. In: Zeigler-Hill V., Shackelford T. (eds) *Encyclopedia of Personality and Individual Differences*. Springer, Cham

18. NBC News Better, Published online, April 26, 2019. By Julie Compton, www.nbcnews.com/better/lifestyle/are-you-chronic-complainer-here-s-how-complaint-cleanse-can-ncna994031

19. https://carolkinseygoman.com

20. Schroeder, Juliana, Jane L. Risen, Francesca Gino, and Michael I. Norton. "Handshaking Promotes Deal-Making by Signalling

Cooperative Intent." *Journal of Personality and Social Psychology 116*, no. 5 (May 2019): 743–768.

21. Goman, Carol Kinsey, "10 Change Leadership Tips Backed By Science", https://carolkinseygoman.com/10-change-leadership-tips-backed-science

22. Laura Martinez, Virginia B. Falvello, Hillel Aviezer & Alexander Todorov (2016) "Contributions of facial expressions and body language to the rapid perception of dynamic emotions", *Cognition and Emotion*, 30:5, 939-952, DOI: 10.1080/02699931.2015.1035229

23. Kraus, Michael W., "Voice-Only Communication Enhances Empathic Accuracy", Yale University, School of Management.

24. 20 August 2018, Leibowitz, K.A., Hardebeck, E.J., Goyer, J.P. et al. J GEN INTERN MED (2018) 33: 2051, https://doi.org/10.1007/s11606-018-4627-z

25. Lipsitz, A. , Kallmeyer, K. , Ferguson, M. and Abas, A. (1989), Counting On Blood Donors: Increasing the Impact of Reminder Calls. *Journal of Applied Social Psychology*, 19: 1057-1067. doi:10.1111/j.1559-1816.1989.tb01239.x

26. Professor Colin McLeod – Program Director, Master of Entrepreneurship in the Faculty of Business and Economics at University of Melbourne, Pursuit, WHY ARE AUSTRALIAN START-UPS FAILING?, https://pursuit.unimelb.edu.au/articles/why-are-australian-start-ups-failing

27. *The Gazette*, Jessica Cohen, published online Jan 4, 2019, www.recordonline.com/news/20190104/world-archery-champ-imparts-art-of-hitting-bullseye

28. BrightLocal.com, www.brightlocal.com/wp-content/uploads/2017/09/best-keywords-for-voice-search.jpg

29. Retail Biz, "HisSmile Capitalising on Social Media to Grow a 100m Brand", Published online by Georgia Clark, September 2018, www.retailbiz.com.au/retail-profiles/hismile-capitalising-on-social-media-to-grow-a-100m-brand

30. Customer Experience Insight, Published online by Michele McGovern, April 9, 2018, www.customerexperienceinsight.com/the-nicest-things-you-can-say-to-customers/

31. Dimensional Research® – Executive Summary, Customer Service and Business Results, Sponsored By ZenDesk. April 2013, www.dimensionalresearch.com

32. Ibid

33. BrightLocal, *Local Consumer Review Survey, written by Rosie Murphy*. Published online December 11, 2019. www.brightlocal.com/research/local-consumer-review-survey

34. BrightLocal, *Local Consumer Review Survey, written by Rosie Murphy*. Published online December 11, 2019. www.brightlocal.com/research/local-consumer-review-survey

35. *Financial Post*, "12 fascinating examples of how apple product placement rules Hollywood", published online August 11, 2012, https://business.financialpost.com/business-insider/12-fascinating-examples-of-how-apple-product-placements-rule-hollywood

36. Weingarten, Gene, "Pearls Before Breakfast" *The Washington Post*, April 8, 2007 Page W10.

Except on Page 95 "Does your dog bite?" was taken from YouTube from *The Pink Panther Strikes Again* movie (1976). Original movie by Amjo Productions, Distributed by United Artists.

BOOK REFERENCES
(AND RECOMMENDED READING)

———————

Allen, James, 1864-1912. *As a Man Thinketh*. Mount Vernon, N.Y.: Peter Pauper Press, 1951.

B., Robert, and Robert B. *Influence (rev)*. Harper Collins, 1993, Harper Collins, 1993.

B., Robert. *Influence: Pearson New International Edition*. Pearson Higher Ed, 2013, Pearson Higher Ed, 2013.

Branham, Leigh, (2012). *The 7 Hidden Reasons Employees Leave: How to Recognize the Subtle Signs and Act Before It's Too Late*, American Management Association, USA.

Burchard, Brendan, *High Performance Habits*, Hay House, 2017.

Burg, Bob and John David. Mann. 2007. *The Go-giver: A Little Story About a Powerful Business Idea*. New York, N.Y.: Portfolio.

Brown, Brené. *Braving the Wilderness: The Quest for True Belonging and the Courage to Stand Alone*. New York: Random House, 2017.

Brown, Brené. *Daring Greatly: How the Courage to Be Vulnerable Transforms the Way We Live, Love, Parent, and Lead*. New York: Gotham Books, 2012.

Cialdini, R. B. (2001). *Influence: Science and practice (4th ed.)*. Boston: Allyn & Bacon.

Damasio, Antonio, (2005). *Decartes' Error*, Penguin Books; Reprint edition (1 September 2005)

Frankl, Viktor E. *Man's Search for Meaning: An Introduction to Logotherapy*. New York: Simon & Schuster, 1984. Print.

Goman, Ph.D., Carol Kinsey, *The Silent Language of Leaders: How Body Language Can Help--or Hurt--How You Lead* - Kindle Edition, Jossey-Bass — a Wiley Imprint, 2011.

Lomenick, Brad. *H3 Leadership: Be Humble. Stay Hungry. Always Hustle.* Harper Collins Leadership, 2015.

Newberg, Andrew, and Mark Robert. *Words Can Change Your Brain*. Penguin, 2012.

Neumeier, Marty, (2006). *ZAG : The #1 Strategy of High-Performance Brands*. Publisher Pearson Education (US), Imprint New Riders Publishing, Berkeley, CA, United States.

Robbins, Anthony. 1992. *Awaken the giant within: how to take immediate control of your mental, emotional, physical & financial destiny!* New York: Simon & Schuster.

Sinek, Simon. *Start With Why*. Penguin UK, 2011.

Suby, Sabri, (2019). *Sell Like Crazy*, Australia. Imprint: Suby Sabri.

Tickle, Naomi, *You Can Read a Face Like a Book: How Reading Faces Helps You Succeed in Business and Relationships*. Daniels Pub, 2003.

Tracy, Brain, (2017). *Million Dollar Habits : Proven Power Practices to Double and Triple Your Income*, Entrepreneur Press, Irvine, United States.

Winch, Guy Dr. *The Squeaky Wheel: Complaining the Right Way to Get Results, Improve Your Relationships, and Enhance Self-Esteem*, Walker & Company, 2011.

www.ingramcontent.com/pod-product-compliance
Lightning Source LLC
Chambersburg PA
CBHW070118110526
44587CB00014BA/1732